Making Problems, Creating Solutions

The person
who says it
cannot be done
should not
interrupt the
person doing it.

—*Chinese Proverb*

MAKING PROBLEMS, CREATING SOLUTIONS

Challenging Young Mathematicians

JILL OSTROW

Foreword by Allyn Snider

Stenhouse Publishers
Portland, Maine

Stenhouse Publishers
www.stenhouse.com

Library of Congress Cataloging-in-Publication Data
Ostrow, Jill.
Making problems, creating solutions : challenging young mathematicians /
Jill Ostrow ; foreword by Allyn Snider.
p.   cm.
Includes bibliographical references.
ISBN 1-57110-041-5 (alk. paper)
1. Mathematics—Study and teaching. 2. Mathematics—Study and teaching
—Activity programs. I. Title.
QA135.5.083   1999
372.7'044—DC21   98-26806 CIP

Cover and interior design by Cathy Hawkes/Cat and Mouse
Cover and interior photographs by Jim Whitney
Illustrations by Alice Cotton

Manufactured in the United States of America on acid-free paper
04 03 02   9 8 7 6 5 4 3 2

To Kyle and Ruth,
two of my best teachers

Contents

Foreword

Problem solving should be the central focus of the mathematics curriculum. As such, it is a primary goal of all mathematics instruction and an integral part of all mathematical activity. Problem solving is not a distinct topic but a process that should permeate the entire program and provide the context in which concepts and skills can be learned.

—NCTM Curriculum Standards

In 1989 the National Council of Teachers of Mathematics (NCTM) came out with a new set of standards for kindergarten through high school. They listed thirteen instructional strands for the early grades, including "Mathematics as Communication," "Mathematical Connections," "Estimation," "Number Sense and Numeration," "Geometry and Spatial Sense," and so on. It took me several years to realize that the first four standards had to do with methodology—the "how" of teaching—and that the last nine had to do with specific content. It took me another year or two to figure out why problem solving wasn't listed in the second part of the list, along with the other content strands. In what ways, I wondered, was problem solving so different from measurement or statistics? I'd always devoted at least one day a week to problem solving in my own classroom, hunting through Marilyn Burns's books for great new ideas and enjoying time away from the standard routines of teaching computation and "applications" (time, money, shapes, graphing, and the like).

Finally, in my quest to make problem solving more integral to daily math instruction, I decided to get down to basics. Just what was a problem, anyway? Dr. Mike Arcidiacono, a professor of math education at Portland State University, explained that a problem was any situation in which the solution wasn't immediately obvious to the problem solver. Something as simple as "Six bears—how many ears?" might pose a genuine problem to many kindergartners while "Sixty-eight wheels in the parking lot—how many cars?" might stump most second graders. Any situation in which children invent their own methods by bringing prior knowledge and skills into play constitutes a problem.

Back in the classroom, it soon became apparent that nearly any mathematical situation, including straight computation, could be used as a source of problem solving, as long as I was willing to pose the problem without teaching the solution method first. Something as simple as double-digit subtraction became a rich source of problem solving in my first/second-grade class and offered me many windows into children's understandings of place value, provided that they were allowed to invent their own methods. When I posed such problems midyear, I wasn't too surprised to see some of my students making tally marks and crossing them out at first—one-by-one counting was tedious, but it almost always worked. As they searched for more efficient methods, some used base 10 blocks or sketches while others began to use such strategies as rounding up or taking the numbers apart and then putting them back together. "43 – 18? Let's see. 43 – 20 would be 23, so the answer must be 25," said some. "43 – 10 is 33, and 33 – 8 is 25," proposed others. A few even used negative numbers in their arguments, ignoring the first rule of elementary double-digit subtraction ("3 – 8 is impossible!" "Not so," they said. "It's –5!"). As their strategies progressed from counting to more sophisticated algorithms, my students seemed more engaged and more empowered. Their comprehension of place value was far greater than it had been when I'd simply taught them to carry and borrow.

About the time I took the plunge into problem solving as a vehicle for teaching and learning, I met Jill Ostrow. She'd been hired to teach first grade while I'd been away at graduate school, but she had moved to a first/second grade by the time I returned. At first I didn't pay much attention. The hallway around her classroom was filled with child-made posters and signs, hung slightly askew at kids'-eye level. The interior decor was casual and cozy, furnished with secondhand couches, coffee tables, cushions, and of course, millions of books. There were these crazy cardboard palm trees stretching to the ceiling, and funny little paper huts and caves spun around some of the desks. I started watching a little more carefully about the time the wooden platform arrived, though. Somehow she and the children managed to build and carpet a three-tiered set of stairs wide enough to sit on. This platform ran around one end of her room and was both elegant and functional and quite sturdy. As she described how they'd managed to design and draw plans for this structure, find people to build it for them, and get the carpeting donated and installed by a local business, I realized that I was in the presence of creative genius.

We started talking and exchanging ideas. It wasn't long before our students were writing story problems for each other and trading strategies back and forth. Eventually, I proposed a switch. Would she take my kids for some work on fractions and let me take hers for a unit on large-scale computation? She agreed and I spent an hour a day in her classroom and she in mine for two consecutive weeks. Her students, I discovered, ranged all the way from a couple of slow, troubled second graders to a tiny first-grade genius; just about the mixed-nut assortment you'd expect to find in our semi-rural, mostly working-class school. They were a respectful but scrappy lot, more resourceful than most, and united in an unusual sort of ownership of their classroom and school. They appeared to be tremendously adept at solving problems of all sorts and probably could have done most things without me. Marinated in Jill's unique blend of trust and high expectations for two years, the second graders were exceptionally self-sufficient, and the first graders followed willingly in their wake.

Life took me to a different school the following year, but the time I'd spent with Jill and her students changed the course of my teaching in many ways. While I wish that every teacher had the chance to spend a few career-altering months in her classroom, I'm hoping that Jill's book will provide a similar opportunity to watch a master teacher in action. *Making Problems, Creating Solutions* sets the foundations for a new way of teaching and learning mathematics. The book provides detailed descriptions of the types of lessons Jill teaches, the sorts of problems she poses, the principles behind her methods, the physical arrangements she uses in her classroom to promote effective teaching and learning, and the ways in which she continually assesses student growth. By filling each chapter with vignettes drawn from her years in first/second-, first- through third-, and fourth- through sixth-grade classrooms, Jill allows us to look over her shoulder and get a sense of how this stuff works with real live kids. While it's not an activity manual or a teacher's guide, *Making Problems, Creating Solutions* offers enough detail to be useful for teachers who want to try some of these ideas in their own classrooms.

So who else should read this book? People who are just starting out, setting up new classrooms and eager to employ the most effective methods of teaching math. Experienced teachers who are looking to change or seeking support for some of the changes they've already made in the direction of standards-based mathematics. Folks who have been using such alternative programs as *Math Their Way, Box It or Bag It Mathematics, Everyday Math, Cognitively Guided Instruction* or *Investigations* and are searching for new extensions or a little more independence. Teachers who have tried, shared, and invented new ideas in literacy and are looking for a parallel universe in math. Anyone who wants to see constructivist theory well applied in a public school setting with children who represent a pretty typical cross section of the American population. Researchers who are interested in children's mathematical thinking. College instructors who want to offer their preservice students a look at the NCTM Standards in action. In short, nearly anyone interested in good educational practices for elementary-aged children would be well advised to spend some time getting to know Jill and her students. Happy reading!

Allyn Snider

Acknowledgments

My students have taught me how brilliant young mathematicians are. To them, I am indebted; thank you.

A special thanks to the following people:

Julia Peattie and Kathy Ostrow, for reading early drafts and offering opinions and suggestions.

Laura Merrill, for being the first person who taught me to think like a mathematician.

All the wonderful supportive parents whose children I have had the privilege to learn with, especially Sherry Parker, Kathy Gregg, Anne Lebwohl, and Laurie Hollander.

My supportive colleagues and friends, especially Kirstin Tonningson, Andra Maklar, Brenda Power, and my Portland Teacher Research group.

Jim Whitney, not only for his amazing photographs but also for his knowledge and excitement about how children learn.

Alice Cotton, for her beautiful illustrations, her friendship, and her wonderful sense of humor.

Ruth Hubbard, for getting me into this whole writing thing. Her enthusiasm is truly inspiring.

Allyn Snider, for reading the manuscript and challenging my words. I have learned so much from this incredible genius.

Aisha Munira, for sharing her mathematical gifts with me and my students. She is the ultimate mathematician and gives new meaning to that title.

The folks at Stenhouse:

Martha Drury, for her attention to detail and expert eye for design.

Tom Seavey . . . almighty promotion guy.

Philippa Stratton, for her willingness to accept all my calls. What support I have from this woman!

Always Grey Wolfe and Howard Waskow, who are constantly teaching me.

Of course Mom and Dad, for all those problems I gave them to solve!

And to Rob, for supporting my decision to take the year off to write and all the craziness that entailed.

Not Just the Facts, Ma'am

Mathematics instruction often is approached in terms of stating and exemplifying rules—the "tell, show, and do" model. Based on the assumption that information can be presented by telling and that understanding will result from being told, such an approach does not work because it frequently overlooks two crucial developmental components: the process of assimilation and the issue of readiness. Essentially, in this approach, students are "ready" intellectually when the teacher is ready for them to receive the information. Learning through such an approach often fails to promote a transfer of mathematical information to new situations.

—NCTM Curriculum Standards

Whoa. That was fast! How did you solve this so quickly?" I asked eight-year-old Kyle one morning during math workshop.

"Well, because it wasn't that hard for me," he replied.

"Yeah, I can see that. But, *how* did you solve it?"

"Well, all this problem wanted to know basically was what 7×8 is. So I got 56," he said.

"OK, but how did you *know* 7×8 was 56 so quickly, and how did you know it was 7×8?" I pushed.

"Well, I knew it was 7×8 because it was an array. The problem asked about a size of a rug that was 7 feet on one side and 8 feet on another side. It wanted to know how many square feet that would be. I knew that it was like an array, so I just times-ed the one side by the other and got 56. Well, actually, 56 *square feet*."

"Great. Can you also explain to me how you came up with 56 so quickly?"

"Yeah, that was the easy part! I know that there are seven points in a touchdown, so I just pretended that there were eight touchdowns. That would be 56 points. Then I just stuck the square feet on the end. That's all I did," he answered.

It might not sound very remarkable that an eight-year-old can multiply two single-digit numbers. It's not. What I do find revealing is the method being used. Kyle's ability to identify a problem and solve it easily has to do with the fact that he has been encouraged to develop his own strategies and explain those strategies to me and to his classmates.

Kyle had never been quizzed, tested, or pushed to learn his math facts quickly. (By *math facts* I mean the traditional multiplication tables and their equivalents for addition, subtraction, and division.) Instead, he had been asked to create strategies for learning the math facts on his own. He had been asked to explain how he knows how to multiply. He had been encouraged to think like a mathematician, to work toward an understanding of what he is learning.

Process Learning

When children are becoming readers, we want them to think like readers. We want our students to learn how to choose appropriate reading material, challenge themselves, and understand what they are reading. We want readers who read for meaning, not machines who read words without comprehending what was read. Isn't that what we want for young mathematicians as well? Allyn Snider and Donna Burk, in their book *Posing and Solving Problems with Story Boxes*, write,

> Many of us who are teachers have come to accept the idea that reading can't really be "taught." We can read to children. As experienced users of print, we can model such strategies as moving our eyes from left to right. . . . We can surround our students with print and share our own love of literature. Many of us believe that in the end, children must sort reading out for themselves, in much the same way they learn [oral] language.
>
> Why then is it so difficult to trust that learning mathematics might work the same way?

We know we can't rush a young reader. Teachers are replacing reading textbooks with real literature. Spelling and applied phonics are being fostered through writing workshops. Countless books have been written on the writing and reading processes over the past few years. Teachers have learned to look at children as individuals, to look at the progress they make over time. We as teachers have learned not to compare children with the other children in their class. We have moved away from the notion that all first-grade children should be reading by the end of first grade. We have moved away from the idea that children should spell every word correctly during a draft. We have learned to let children learn rather than drilling them to death. We have learned to focus on the process of learning.

I have been observing young mathematicians for the last 16 years. I have learned from these observations how critical it is for children to progress naturally in their mathematical development, just as they progress naturally in their language development. That is not to say I do not have intentional directions and challenges for my students. I do. I look for progress in each of my students. I don't expect a group of third graders all to be at the same level of understanding and at the same place in their mathematical development by the end of the year. I look at each child's progress over the year. I assess where each child began and where each child ended up.

Young mathematicians need a strong, solid foundation. For me, that foundation is built on understanding, challenge, the ability to share and explain and describe, independence, confidence, and choice.

The foundation is built and reinforced by letting children have time to think, rethink, make errors, experience a wide range of problems to solve, create strategies, and share strategies with each other. When math makes sense to students—when they are able to make connections and have time to experiment with strategies—they will gain a stronger understanding of concepts they are learning. The National Council of Teachers of Mathematics writes, "When mathematics evolves naturally from problem situations that have meaning to children and is regularly related to their environment, it becomes relevant and helps children link their knowledge to many kinds of situations" (1989).

Meaning and purpose should be at the core of any mathematics program. Something that has become a very powerful notion to me is that children can explore without being taught specific procedures. For instance, a young child may be asked to solve the following problem: "There are 28 cookies on the table and seven children. How many cookies will each child get?" The child may solve this using unifix cubes and get the answer that each child will get four cookies. He may not know that the operation for that problem is $28 \div 7 = 4$. In other words, children can solve division problems using the notion of sharing without first needing to internalize the entire concept of division.

I have also discovered that children can divide, for instance, without first knowing how to add, subtract, or multiply. Young children are capable of doing problems that we have traditionally thought of as too challenging. Curriculum goals tend to follow an old belief that there is a specific order of learning. Because of these curriculum guides, we teachers of young children believed that children must learn addition, then subtraction, then multiplication, and so on. I have found this to be not only inaccurate but sometimes even a disservice to students. My youngest children actually find division much easier to understand than subtraction. Yet as elementary teachers we were taught to stick to a set sequence. Just as children need to be surrounded by all types of literature, children need to be surrounded by all types of mathematical concepts.

If we begin to look at mathematics as a type of language, perhaps mathematics education can begin to be restructured. Instead of looking at the parts and going to the whole, we need to look at the whole and include the parts. We can look at mathematics education as using a *process-driven curriculum* rather than a set of specifically sequenced concepts.

Becoming Mathematicians

Understanding is the key to becoming a mathematician. Understanding what a problem is asking, understanding how to come up with a strategy to solve the problem, understanding enough to write or draw in detail how to solve the problem—these are crucial to becoming a competent and confident mathematician.

I am a reader and a writer, but I did not consider myself a mathematician until a few years ago. My good friend and colleague Aisha Munira helped me to see myself as a mathematician. She showed me how to *understand* what I had been taught in elementary school. I had never understood fractions and couldn't for the life of me explain how dividing fractions worked. She showed me how to look at fractions in a new way, to use manipulatives and graph paper to really look at what I was working on. I remember when I learned how to divide fractions using a visual model. I can't tell you how excited I was! From there, everything I presented to my students I relearned; and I discovered what I had missed in my education as a child. It wasn't that I couldn't do the operations or the equations, but I didn't understand what I was doing or how they worked. Aisha is a mathematician. She teaches children by respecting them as mathematicians.

Along with teaching college math courses and working with children, Aisha also teaches workshops through the Math Learning Center (MLC), a nonprofit organization in Portland, Oregon. The philosophy driving the MLC programs and curricula is similar to Aisha's and mine; and they reflect the fundamentals of math reform. The MLC publications *Opening Eyes to Mathematics* (Arcidiacono, Head, and Pollett 1995) and *Visual Mathematics* (Bennett and Foreman 1995) were very helpful to me in my teaching—the former for grades 1–3 and the latter for older classes. A new MLC curriculum, *Bridges to Mathematics,* by Allyn Snider and Donna Burk, is in preparation for the K–2 grade levels.

You will be reading about Aisha often in this book. I called on her to help me when I began teaching a new combined class of fourth, fifth, and sixth graders. I knew I would be able to go through the curriculum and teach them what they needed to learn. But I wanted them to get a deeper understanding of what they were learning, and I knew that if I understood more they would too. I had been teaching the lower elementary grades for so long that I was afraid I had forgotten much of what happens in the upper grades. I'm not shy about admitting to my mathematical shortcomings! So Aisha came into our room from January to May twice a week during our math workshop to work with me and my students on some of the more complex mathematical ideas that I had lost. When Aisha came in, I didn't leave; instead, I became a student. I did the work my students were doing, participated in groups and partnerships, and contributed to discussions.

I moved freely and comfortably between being a student and being a teacher during that time. I learned not just skills but more—how older children think like younger children. What I had discovered about time, practice, sharing, and exploration of ideas with my younger students was just as important for my older ones. Just because the concepts and skills were different with the older children, the way I approached their learning could be the same. In other words, the mathematical foundation that I had discovered to be so crucial with young children was just as crucial for my older classes.

I also reaffirmed my belief that it's not only OK but vital for teachers to learn right alongside their students. And I learned how much I already knew about teaching.

This is *not* an activity book. This is *not* a book about teaching math in a multiage classroom. It *is* a book about what I have learned about the mathematical process and thinking from the six- to twelve-year-old children with whom I've worked. This book goes beyond the usual curriculum goals in that I believe these goals underestimate what kids are really capable of doing.

Children need a strong foundation first and foremost. During math workshop, they build on that foundation by actively practicing what they are learning. They work on integrated projects that pull together what they have practiced. They present what they have learned, and I assess their progress by looking at their work. The skills, concepts, district guidelines, and NCTM Standards fit into this structure of foundation, practice, and assessment. Throughout this book you will be reading how foundation, practice, and assessment form the core of my math program.

Mathematicians in the Making

Students will perform better and learn more in a caring environment in which they feel free to explore mathematical ideas, ask questions, discuss their ideas, and make mistakes. By listening to students' ideas and encouraging them to listen to one another, one can establish an atmosphere of mutual respect. Teachers can foster this willingness to share by helping students explore a variety of ideas in reaching solutions and verifying their own thinking. This approach instills in students an understanding of the value of independent learning and judgment and discourages them from relying on an outside authority to tell them whether they are right or wrong.

—*NCTM Curriculum Standards*

I t's more important to understand how you did something than to just get a right answer," said nine-year-old Kyle. Kyle knows a lot about becoming a mathematician. He understands the importance of *understanding* math. He understands that while it is important to be accurate, without understanding answers are just answers.

Becoming a mathematician means learning how to understand what you are being asked to do. It's not about coming up with right answers. Adult mathematicians often work on problems for years and years. They work through thinking strategies, take time to rethink, make mistakes, and keep working toward understanding. Children need time to become mathematicians. They need time to work through problems to gain understanding. It's not a quick fix. Just because a student can solve an equation doesn't mean she understands the equation.

It takes time to understand any mathematical concept. This sounds so simple, doesn't it? But it seems as though we educators rush kids through concepts so quickly that they become something to *do* rather than something to understand.

Children need time to think through problems they are given. They need to be able to create and use their own strategies as they solve problems. I remember Josh as a first grader. I would give out a problem, and he would sit for such a long time that I often wondered if he was working. I came to realize he just needed thinking time. Even as a sixth grader, he took time to sit and think about a problem before he began to work on a solution, unlike Carly, who jumped right in with her various solutions. All children approach problem solving in different ways.

The word *problem* is defined in the dictionary as "any question or matter involving doubt, uncertainty, or difficulty; a question proposed for solution or discussion." In other words, something that can't be easily solved, or something that involves some sort of questioning and discussion. I look for these qualities when I write problems for my students. I want my problems to be challenging, to provoke discussion, and even (and I tell this to my students) to cause frustration. How can a real problem not cause frustration?

I am not afraid to let my students become frustrated. When they are tackling a difficult problem is a time for children to rethink, reflect, and work. The problems my children work on are messy; they require thinking and rethinking, and time.

Where do I get the problems I give to my students? I usually write them myself. I draw upon what I have learned from Allyn Snider, Marilyn Burns, Aisha Munira, and a host of books I have found helpful. I also write problems based on what I have learned over the years from my students: besides the actual problems, I have learned *how* my students solve problems.

Children need to be able to use a variety of problem-solving strategies. I assume my students will use manipulatives, drawings and pictures, invented algorithms, and any other problem-solving strategies they can come up with. I have watched my young students use drawings to help them understand concepts and solve problems, and pictures are just as important to show understanding with older students. Aisha and I would often ask the kids to use pictures as an assessment for understanding.

Alex, a fifth grader, was used to solving problems using algorithms that were taught to him in the earlier grades. He would solve problems rather quickly, yet at times I would question his understanding. I frequently asked Alex to explain his solution with a drawing along with his written description. Knowing Alex, and knowing his capabilities, I could ask him to go further to demonstrate his understanding. I believe that, with some children, if they can't show it, they don't understand it. For example, the following problem was quite simple for Alex: "Six people want to split five pies equally among themselves. How much pie does each get?" Alex quickly wrote down 5/6 in his journal.

"That was easy," he said.

"Was it? Well, why don't you do a drawing explaining your answer," I said. And, as always, he grunted at me and went off to draw his picture of five circles split into six pieces with one piece shaded in each circle. Even with this simple problem that he solved quickly in his head, coming up with the drawing posed a new challenge for him. Asking children, especially older children who are used to just giving number answers, to show their work with a drawing furthers their understanding. By using drawings and diagrams to show thinking strategies, students get a deeper understanding of what they are learning. Alex understood his answer, but I questioned whether he understood his process. Having him draw his solution was not only helpful to me to see his thinking process, it was helpful to him as well.

During one math workshop, Dave chose to multiply 97×68. He showed how he used a traditional algorithm as well as how he used a visual model for multiplication. His written explanation follows:

> How I did it: Algorithm—First I did 8×7, and got 56. I carried the 5 and put down the 6. Then, I did $8 \times 9 + 5$ and got 77. The answer is 776. For the second one, I brought down a zero because you're going to the tens. Then did 6×7. It was 42. I carried the 4 and put down the 2. Then I did $6 \times 9 + 4$ and I got 5820. I plussed 5820 and 776 and got 6596.
>
> The array—I pretended that one side of a square is 10. So I went over 9 squares and 7 tiny dots. I went down 6 squares and 8 tiny dots. I found all the arrays, then added them up. I got 6596.

Kyle had had an extremely interesting way of adding numbers mentally ever since first grade. He could never quite explain to me how his process worked. Well, actually, his explanations were quite accurate; it was I who couldn't follow his thinking. When he was a third grader, I asked him to explain exactly how he added the numbers $87 + 76$, and he simply wrote, "163," so I questioned him some more.

"Kyle," I urged, "please try to explain how you do this so I can understand it. Maybe use a picture." Here is what he came up with.

He drew what went on in his brain by drawing his brain! It was easy for me to see that he was thinking.

As Kyle says, it's more important to understand than to just get the right answer. By building a foundation for mathematicians, and giving them a variety of mathematical situations and experiences, children can understand what they are learning.

1

Building a Foundation

I wonder why it is so easy to accept differences in strategies in reading and writing but so difficult to accept differences in solving equations. I do not teach my students in any grade to carry and borrow using the traditional algorithm most of us were taught. In her book *About Teaching Mathematics*, Marilyn Burns writes,

> It's important for children to understand that one particular algorithm may be no better or more efficient than another, and that many methods, including ones they invent themselves, are equally valid. There is no need for all students to do arithmetic calculations in the same way any more than it is essential for all children to develop identical handwritings or writing styles.

When I look at how Kyle solves equations, I am in awe of his mathematical creativity, his understanding of number. I believe that if I had taught him how to carry and borrow the way I had been taught, I would not only have confused him but would have done him an injustice. Constance Kamii, who has done extensive research in this area, writes, "When children invent their own ways, (1) they do not have to give up their own thinking; (2) their understanding of place value is strengthened; (3) they develop better number sense."

I read many articles about why it's important to let kids create their own algorithms. But it wasn't until I observed my students creating their own that I understood how significant my decision to stop teaching traditional algorithms was.

The foundation for making mathematicians is to create an environment where children can practice what they are learning. It's about welcoming and expecting different learning styles. It's about making room for the huge

11

range of ability levels. Building a foundation for mathematicians is about respecting children enough to let them learn and creating an environment that is safe and comfortable for children to try out new methods and ideas. An environment where children can take time to think about problems they are working on, share their strategies, and build on their problem-solving strategies is first and foremost. I want my kids to focus on how they are solving problems, what strategies they are creating for themselves.

When I began to observe my students creating algorithms (multistep procedures such as carrying and borrowing), I learned to look at the *process* they were working through before looking at the answer. This was hard for me to do at first. I was used to looking at the answer first. But after I observed what they were capable of, and what their strategies were, I relaxed. I noticed my students were mathematicians, not just equation solvers. Letting go of teaching traditional algorithms opened the door for me to look at all aspects of how children become mathematicians.

Children work on editing and revising in order to get their pieces ready to be read by an audience. Math is no different. If kids don't have the opportunity to practice, make mistakes, create strategies, ask questions, and share, they are missing a huge part of becoming competent mathematicians. Children who are asked to spit out answers to equations can do just that. But ask them to explain their thinking strategies or to solve the problem in a different way, and they look lost.

When I first asked Alex to explain how he solved a problem he had just completed, he was stymied. He was very quick, competent, and accurate at solving complex equations, but he couldn't explain why or how the equation worked. He knew he was good at math and would often write, "I did it in my head. I don't know how I did it. I just did." One day I said to him, "Alex, if you can't explain how you came up with your solution, I guess you don't understand what you are doing." That was too much for him! He began to think about steps he was taking, and he even learned to make drawings to help with his explanations. I believe Alex is a better mathematician because of this.

One morning, seven-year-old Jacob was observing a fifth-grade teacher showing me a visual model for multiplying fractions. "This is cool, Jill," he said. "Look how easy it is. All you need to do is to draw these boxes." He began to play around with the model during math workshop. I would not, however, interpret that to mean he fully understood the concept of multiplying fractions. What I could say is that he did not have a fear of numbers, was willing and able to play around with visual models for mathematics, could explain how he solved a problem, and knew he had the time to explore such concepts and ideas.

JACOB'S SOLUTION FOR $\frac{3}{4} \times \frac{4}{5}$

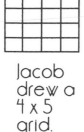

Jacob drew a 4 x 5 grid.

He shaded in $\frac{3}{4}$.

Then, he shaded in $\frac{4}{5}$.

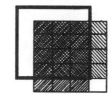

Jacob drew a box around the overlapping array which gave him an answer of $\frac{12}{20}$.

The year I was teaching fourth, fifth, and sixth graders, my students were multiplying fractions using the same visual model that Jacob played with as a first grader. The older students were able to figure out how and why the visual model worked. They were also able to transfer the model to real problem-solving situations. I had to restrain myself from telling them, "Look! It's so easy to multiply fractions. Just multiply across. Can't you see that?" It was hard to let them use the visual model and take all that time to draw boxes when the traditional algorithm was so much easier. But when Dave discovered that way for himself, I felt it had been worth my patience. He was working on several problems when I overheard him talking with his group. Then he and several other children came up to me, and he said, "Hey, Jill, look! All you have to do is multiply across the top and then the bottom, and you get the same answer as with the pictures."

"That's pretty cool, Dave," I said. "How about sharing your discovery with the whole class." So we had a group discussion and talked about why the model works, whether it works every time, and what it means to multiply fractions. They came to the same place they would have reached if I had told them how to do it the way I had learned, and it certainly would have been faster, but what's the rush? I would much rather have my students discover mathematical solutions on their own and understand what they are doing. What better assessment for understanding than when a child discovers a method for solving a problem or a strategy for learning the math facts?

What's the Rush?

Even though I challenge my students, I don't rush them through understanding. If we try to rush mathematical understanding, we just end up confusing children. Why, then, are we still cramming the memorization of math facts down our young students' throats and asking them to know these before they understand what they are memorizing? Again, when I use the term *math facts*, I mean the basic multiplication tables and their equivalents for addition, subtraction, and division.

Facts are important in math, yes, just as sounds are important in language. Yet we have learned that children need exposure to literature and writing for them to become readers and writers. They do not become good readers by memorizing each blend or digraph in a word. Practice, exposure, and real work is how children learn to become readers and writers. Children become mathematicians the same way.

I don't agree with the whole "speed" thing when it comes to mathematical development. I can understand why teachers give their students speed tests on math facts, because that is how it's always been done. We learned this way, and it's the way to get kids to learn their math facts fast. It's a practice that isn't questioned. But I'm asking you to question it.

If children can show me that they understand what a math fact is, if they can show me that they can solve complex problems and explain in detail how they came to their solutions, then they have proved to me they are mathematicians. I'm *not* saying that children shouldn't learn and know their multiplication tables, but I believe we are asking them to memorize these tables before they understand what they are memorizing. Asking children to memorize the times tables in second or third grade seems much too soon.

As children learn new spelling strategies, they begin to memorize spelling patterns. I have found my students to become better spellers in the long run if they are able to create and learn spelling strategies at a young age. As they get older and become more experienced with writing and reading, spelling patterns are memorized. The same holds true for the basic math facts. As children create and share strategies for solving problems, and use the math facts, they will memorize the facts with understanding.

As they share their strategies with one another, children learn about different strategies. During one sharing session, the children were telling how each of them had added two single-digit numbers. Cody showed how he added 4 + 5: "I took four cubes out and then I took five cubes out. Then I went, 1, 2, 3, 4, 5, 6, 7, 8, 9."

"That's great, Cody," I said. "Are there any comments for Cody?"

"Yeah, I have a comment, Cody," said Kyle. "It might be easier if you started to count from 4. I mean, you already know you have four cubes, right? So you could start counting from there instead. It might be faster." He was trying to show Cody how to count on instead of always going back to 1.

"Kyle, can you show Cody what you mean? Actually do it for him?"

"Sure. So you already know you have four, right? So take out five cubes and start counting from there. 5, 6, 7, 8, 9. Like that."

Cody practiced counting on for the rest of the year. It was not an easy strategy for him, but he practiced because he knew it would be a faster strategy. Had he simply memorized 4 + 5, he wouldn't have gone through the process of understanding that he needed to go through.

I am focusing so strongly on the issue of facts and computation because it seems to me that this is still at the core of teachers' concerns when trying to rethink their own math programs. Some of my students may not be able to come out with the answer to 6×9 in seconds flat, but they can explain what 6×9 means and create a strategy for coming up with an answer.

I remember children who came into my room who could rattle off their multiplication tables fast and accurately. Yet when I asked them to show me what 6×9 means, they'd stare at me like I had asked them to solve a calculus problem. I have had children enter my class who could solve problems with no understanding of what their algorithm was. That concerns me. In her book *About Teaching Mathematics*, Marilyn Burns writes,

> Teachers admit to spending more than 75 percent of their math time (closer to 90 percent for many) on paper-and-pencil drill, with students practicing arithmetic skills in isolation from problem-solving situations. The arithmetic exercises are usually provided on worksheets or textbook pages, neatly arranged and ready for children to apply their computation skills to figure answers. Yet, in all real-life needs for arithmetic, problems do not present themselves ready for calculation. Deciding what to do is the important first step before doing any calculation.
>
> Learning to do paper-and-pencil arithmetic on isolated examples does nothing to ensure that children will truly understand the algorithms or develop the ability to use them when needed.

Many teachers have told me that the reason they give drill and practice and speed tests to their students is because the teacher in the next grade will be upset if the kids don't know the math facts. I think I would be more upset if my new group of children could not think like mathematicians . . . could not describe their thinking, could not write about solutions, could not question problems, could not discuss strategies. I'd much rather have a group of kids who could do those things than a group of kids who knew their times tables fast. Can we have both? Yes. But the memorization of facts must be met with understanding, and I have found it more appropriate and useful to ask fifth or sixth graders to memorize facts than to ask second or third graders to do so. If we could just slow down and give younger children the time they need to explore strategies and develop mathematical understanding, I believe they would have a richer and stronger foundation for when we asked them to know the facts. I asked my fourth, fifth, and sixth graders why it was important for them to know their math facts quickly.

"Well, now that I'm older, it helps to do harder problems. Like, I don't have to think too hard about a fact if I know it fast. I can concentrate more on doing the problem and not on trying to figure out the fact," said ten-year-old Tessia.

"I knew all of the times tables in third grade, but I don't think I really knew what I was doing. I mean, I think I understand better now. Even though I didn't know my 8's very well, this year, now that I'm older and have to write about my thinking, I can do them better now," said sixth grader Kim.

It seems that drill is one of the hardest parts of math programs for teachers of young children to let go of. It seems natural to allow kids to explore when it comes to patterning, geometry, spatial thinking, and measurement activities, but when we talk about computation, it's back to teacher-directed activities. It doesn't have to be that way. Children can explore number in a variety of ways. Through sharing, they learn many methods, not just one. There are several ways children practice skills and concepts they are exposed to. When children practice computation by using math facts to solve problems and doing multistep procedures, they gain an understanding of what a fact means, developing a stronger sense of number.

What's Your Method?

Kyle

Kyle was in second grade when I asked him to do a math worksheet for me. I was giving a workshop on mathematical thinking, and I wanted to prove the point that one really cannot assess understanding just from correct answers; one must know the thinking. I showed the audience the worksheet that Kyle had completed, one of those standard math worksheets filled with double-digit addition and subtraction equations. His answers were written under the equations, but he hadn't "shown his work" because there were no carrying or borrowing marks. I asked the group of teachers to tell me, by looking at his worksheet, how Kyle had solved these equations. Following are some of their responses:

"Well, I can't see his work, so I assume he used a calculator."

"He used his fingers?"

"He looked at someone else's page. I can't see any carrying or borrowing marks."

"He used tens strips or manipulatives."

"He doesn't pay attention to the plus and minus signs."

As I was saying no to all these responses, the teachers looked confused. "Well, how did he solve them, then?" they asked.

"As far as I know," I said, "this was the first time he had ever seen a worksheet like this. I asked him to choose two equations—one subtraction and one addition—and write an explanation that I could share with you." I read Kyle's written response:

> What I did for 67 − 39 is I just left 2 from the 39, so that made 37. Then I took 37 away from 67, and that was 30. So then I took away 2 from the extra 2, and that was 28.
>
> How I did 19 + 54 was I put the 4 from the 54 aside and added 20 instead of 19 to 54, and that was 74. And then I took away 1 from 74, and that was 73.

It took a few readings, and finally me doing a drawing on the blackboard, before they understood what Kyle's thinking was. They were amazed at how complex it was.

Megan

For workshops, conferences, and my own research, I often give my students a raw multistep equation to solve. Look at an addition problem that Megan solved (Figure 1.1), and see if you can figure out what she did. This is the algorithm Megan has invented to solve addition equations. I notice several things when I look at this. First, Megan knows about place value. She starts at the left and goes to the right. She added the 4000 and the 3000 and wrote

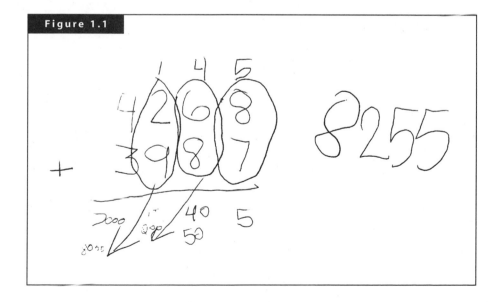

Figure 1.1

7000 below. When I question children who have been taught to carry, they usually tell me that they carried the 1 and put it on top of the next number. Megan knows she isn't really adding 4 + 3 but adding thousands. She then moves right and adds 200 + 900, circling those two numbers. She puts the 1000 from 1100, with the 7000 and writes 8000. (Note the arrow.) She then puts the extra 100 on top of the 200. She continues in this way until she has her solution of 8255.

Young children learn to read from left to right; it is therefore the logical thing for them to do to solve equations from left to right. When children are not taught the traditional addition algorithm, they will usually start from the left. I learned so much by observing my students creating algorithms; it really did make a big impact on me as a teacher. Here are a few more of the different algorithms my young students have invented to add numbers together.

Ross

Ross added 48 + 56 (Figure 1.2). He too started left. He wrote, "I knew that 50 + 40 was 90. Then I added 8 and then 6 and got 104." Again, Ross added 50 and 40, not 5 and 4, showing a solid understanding of place value.

Figure 1.2

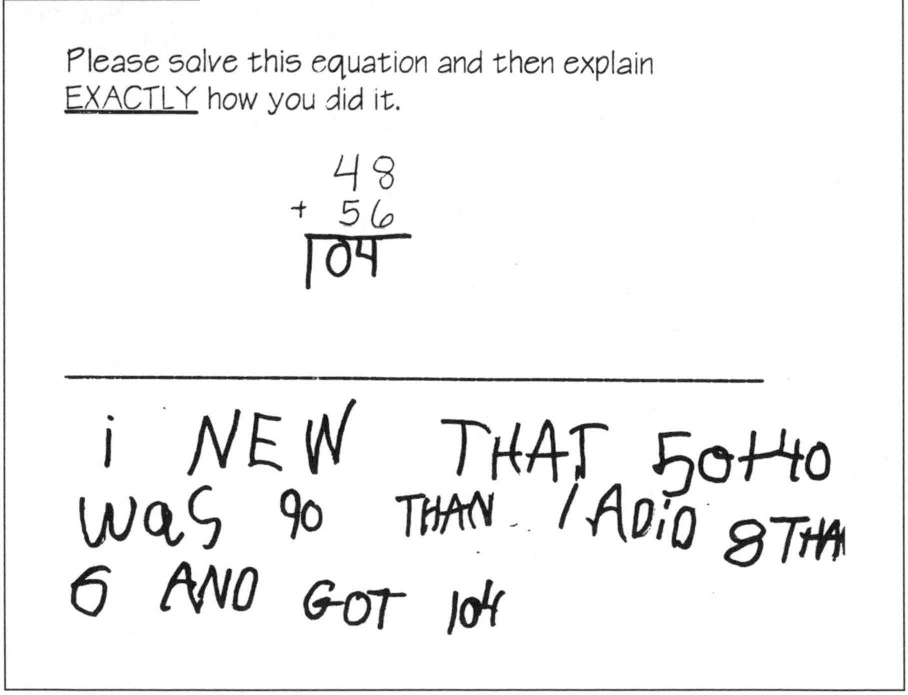

Please solve this equation and then explain EXACTLY how you did it.

$$\begin{array}{r} 4\,8 \\ +\ 5\,6 \\ \hline 104 \end{array}$$

i NEW THAT 50+40 waS 90 THAN I ADID 8 THA 6 AND GOT 104

Jacob

Jacob is an interesting mathematician, and his invented algorithms reflect this. He was asked to add 249 + 73. He wrote, "I added 40 and 70 = 110, + 200 = 310 + 12 = 322." It took me a while to figure out what he had done. Jacob likes to start at the tens. (I remember giving him an equation in the thousands, and he still started with the tens.) So he began by adding the 40 from 249 and the 70 from 73. He then added the 200 to his sum of 40 + 70 to get 310. He then added the 12 he got from adding 9 + 3 and came up with the solution of 322.

Caitlin

As Megan did, Caitlin circled the steps she went through. She was asked to add 586 + 378 (Figure 1.3). She wrote, "OK, I will show you how I did it. [She shows in drawings how she added 500 and 300.] Then, after 800, I circle 80 + 70. That's 150, and then 800 + 150 = 950. Then I circle 6 + 8 = 14,

Figure 1.3

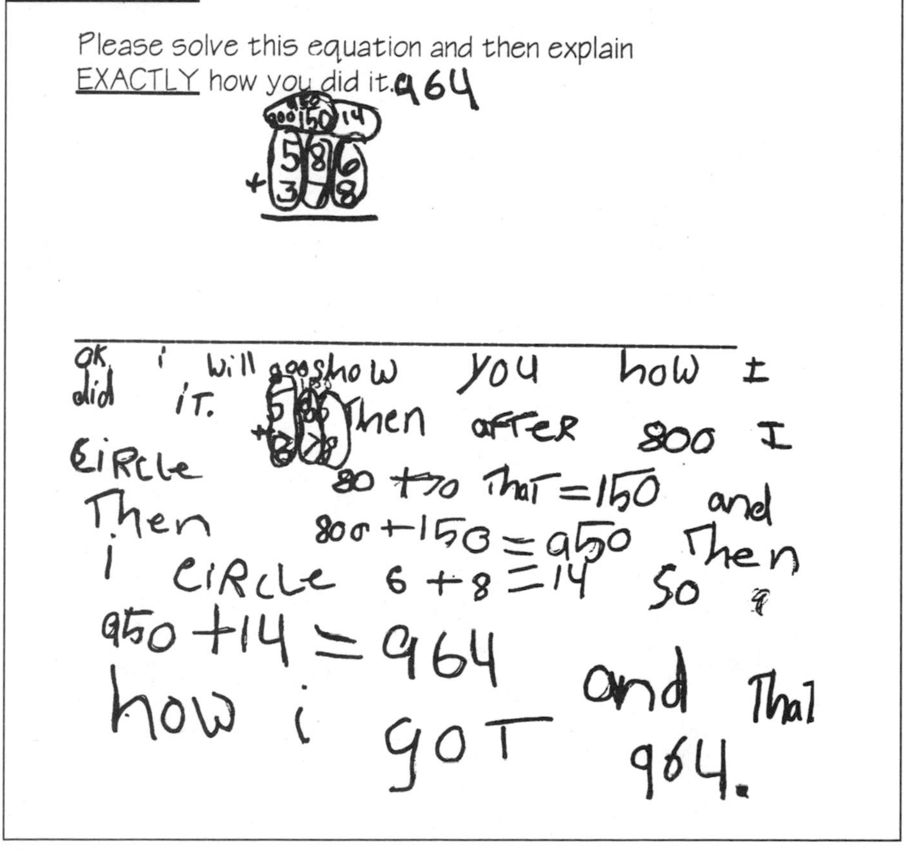

so 950 + 14 = 964, and that's how I got 964." Caitlin wrote the answers on top of the numbers and then added across.

Kyle, Again

Kyle was asked to add 379 + 87 (Figure 1.4). He wrote—and you'll no doubt need to read this a few times to understand what he did—"I just added 30 to 379, and that was 409. Then I added the other 57, and that was 466, and how I got 466 is I took 7 away from 57 and then added 9 to 50, so then it was 59. Then I added the 7, and that was 466." OK, Kyle, whatever you say! Kyle has the most inventive brain, and it really shows as he works mathematically. He always changes numbers to make them easier to add. He does this in his head, unlike some of the other students who circle and keep their work on paper. He added 30 to 379. He got the 30 from taking 30 away from the 87. It was easier for him to add 30 than another number. He knew that if he took 30 away from 87, he would be left with 57. To make adding 57 easier, he added 50 and saved the 7 for the end. Now, if I were asked to add this way, it would take me a fairly long time. It would not be an efficient way for me to add numbers quickly. But for Kyle this is the most efficient method. He does this so quickly, it is difficult to follow him unless he explains it in writing.

Figure 1.4

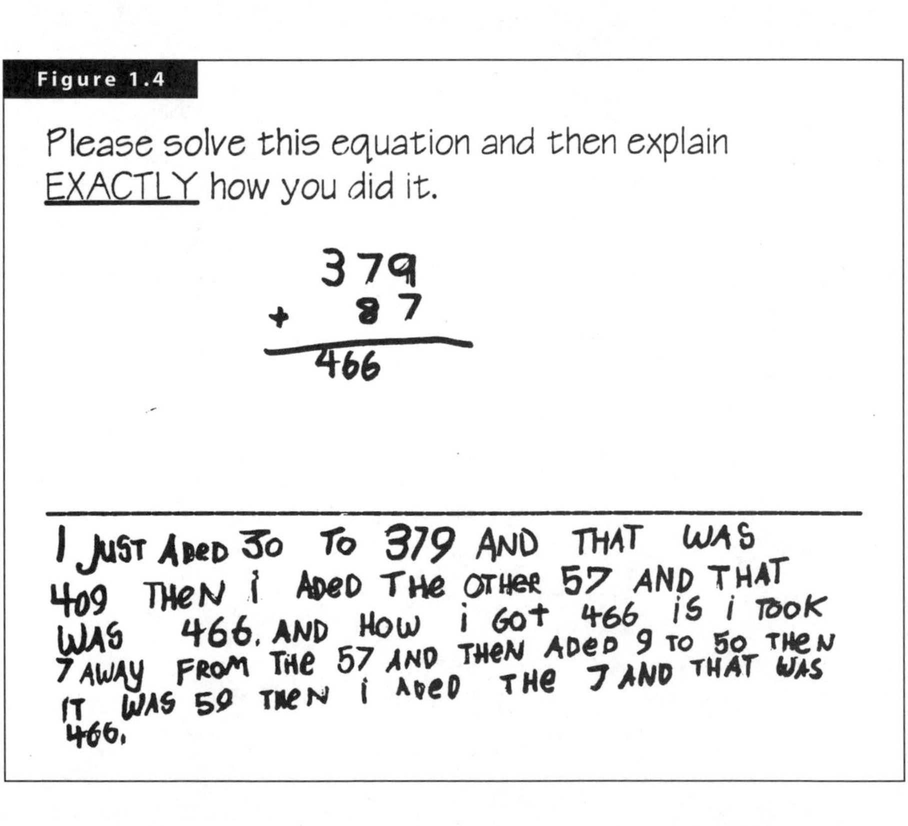

Please solve this equation and then explain
<u>EXACTLY</u> how you did it.

$$\begin{array}{r} 379 \\ +\ 87 \\ \hline 466 \end{array}$$

I JUST ADED 30 TO 379 AND THAT WAS 409 THEN i ADED THE OTHER 57 AND THAT WAS 466. AND HOW i GoT 466 iS i TOoK 7 AWAY FROM THE 57 AND THEN ADED 9 TO 50 THEN IT WAS 59 THEN i ADED THE 7 AND THAT WAS 466.

I think we teach children how to carry because we believe it is the most efficient method of adding numbers, and it *is* an efficient method, yet some of the methods children invent are more efficient for them. Besides, efficient or not, when kids are allowed to invent their own algorithms, they understand better what they are doing.

We share all the methods the kids create in large-group sharing time. The different methods for adding numbers that I just described are only a handful. Each of these children have shared their methods over and over again during sharing time, so they have been introduced and exposed to many different algorithms. When I want to expose them to the conventional algorithm of carrying, it is just another method for them to see. I tell my children that their methods are valid but that some teachers will want them to use this way. It is so much easier for them to accept this after they have been exposed to many other methods. I think we are too quick to show kids the way we were taught. I say, wait, and let them show you the ways they have learned for themselves.

I believe we need to give young children the chance to make sense of numbers on their own first, before they are taught conventional methods. To teach second graders how to carry and borrow before they can even show that they understand the concept of place value seems absurd. When I showed some invented algorithms to a group of graduate interns I taught one summer, they looked confused by all the different ways.

"Now, imagine you are eight years old and I'm showing you how to put this group of ten above that group of ten. Imagine how confusing it is for an eight-year-old" I said.

"What about subtraction?" asked one intern. "How can kids do that?"

I showed them Megan's invented algorithm for subtraction (Figure 1.5) and let them try to figure out what she had done. It was hard for them to

Figure 1.5

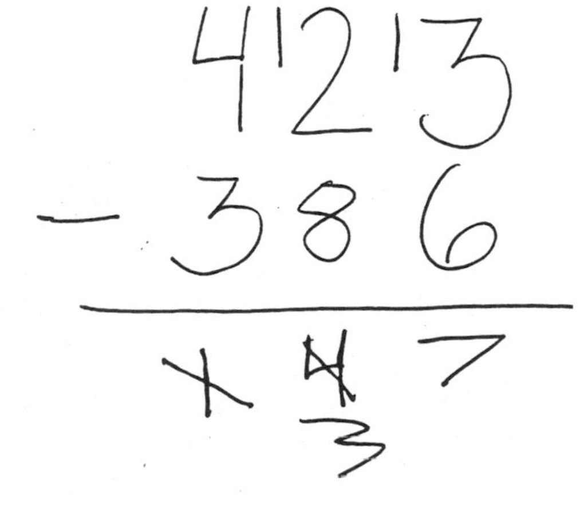

figure out her thinking, so I explained it as best I could. I said that she had subtracted the 300 from the 400 first and had written 1. (Over the years, Megan has found her own shortcuts. She no longer needed to write the zeros, as she had done when she was younger. She knew that this 1 stood for 100.) Then she knew she couldn't take 8 away from 2, so she borrowed from the hundreds place: she crossed out the 1 and included it with the 2, and then she could subtract 8 from 12. Basically, she borrows from the answer, not from the numbers being taken away.

My kids don't just one day come into class and invent an algorithm. They can do this because of the constant practice they get using tens strips and other manipulatives. They transfer to paper what they know about using things, and they are exposed to other strategies during sharing and discussions. When I feel a child is ready to stop using manipulatives for a certain type of equation, I might suggest, "Can you figure out a way to do that without using the strips?" An on-the-spot assessment shows me if they are ready to do that.

Computation is an important part of the mathematical process, just as spelling is an important part of the writing process. But just as we now respect children's invented spellings, we need to also respect children's invented mathematical methods.

Let's Share

I intentionally write problems that encourage collaboration and questioning, require thinking, invite discussion, leave room for uncertainty, and pose a challenge. These are anything but neat and simple. I want my children to work hard, to challenge themselves, to question my solutions, to understand the reasons and rules for their strategies, to argue and discuss solutions, to become frustrated, and to gain confidence and independence as mathematicians.

The problems I write for my students are based on the skills I want to focus on that day—for example, division. The *content* of the problems I often take from what we are studying in other areas. For instance, when we were studying the Arctic, the problems mentioned mukluks and parkas. During our study of World War II, they concerned aspects of the war and the home front.

One year my students wanted to transform our room into a town. They named it Kidsville, and we spent the year building our town and exploring different aspects of Kidsville. That same year, the children wanted to have a real café, a place where other kids from the community could come. We talked about how this could work, and we decided that maybe a local coffee shop would let us hold our café at their shop. A group of children who were interested in starting this wrote a proposal to a few of the coffee shops in town. We had an interview with the owner of one of the shops, and the proposal was accepted. The café was named Kids' Café, and every Wednesday afternoon, from 4 to 5 o'clock, three kids from my class went to the coffee shop with me. They served doughnuts and drinks from behind the counter. We also used this hour to hold readings. Children from the community came to our café and read their pieces of writing. It was such a wonderful way to have children share their work outside of school. It was also a great way for my students to get a glimpse of how a real business was run. At the end of the hour, we counted up the money we had made. We were allowed to keep 50 percent of what our Kids' Café earned. I was able to use the café background in many problems. We would add up the money we had already made, pretend to divide our earnings by 27 to see how much money we could each have, and predict how much we could earn by the end of the year.

I also get ideas from other mathematicians and educators and write variations of their problems. One basic problem I have used for years came, I believe, from Marilyn Burns. I think the original problem that she wrote had to do with animals and legs—something like, If there were five horses, how many legs would there be?

One modification of that problem I wrote was during our study of the Civil War. Figure 1.6 shows the problem and Carly's solution. She solved it by grouping and adding numbers. Melissa used colored tiles. Kyle drew pictures to help himself. When we shared, the whole class got a chance to hear all the varieties of strategies. During sharing time, the children not only heard different strategies but were able to question them as well.

"I drew a picture of the eight union soldiers and then counted the stuff I needed," said Kyle. "Questions or comments?"

"I don't see how you counted the muskets. I don't see them there," said Megan.

"Oh, yeah, well I knew that only half of them had muskets, and half of 8 is 4, so I just wrote 4," he explained.

"I did it sort of like Kyle, but I just drew stick figures. After a while, I could just add it up without looking at the pictures," said Dave.

Sharing strategies and solutions is an essential part of building a mathematical foundation. Kids get ideas from others and learn to question the strategies they hear.

With a problem that asked the kids to figure out what the year would be and how old they would be in 50 years, several strategies were shared.

"Since I'm nine, I just added 9 to 50 and got 59. That was easy," said Carly.

"Why was that easy? What made it easy for you, do you think?" I asked.

"Because it's easy to add small numbers to tens numbers. It's easy for me," she said.

"Does anyone think it isn't easy to do that?"

"I don't," Jack replied.

"Can anyone show Jack a way to add small numbers to tens numbers to make it easy, as Carly says?" I asked the class.

Figure 1.6

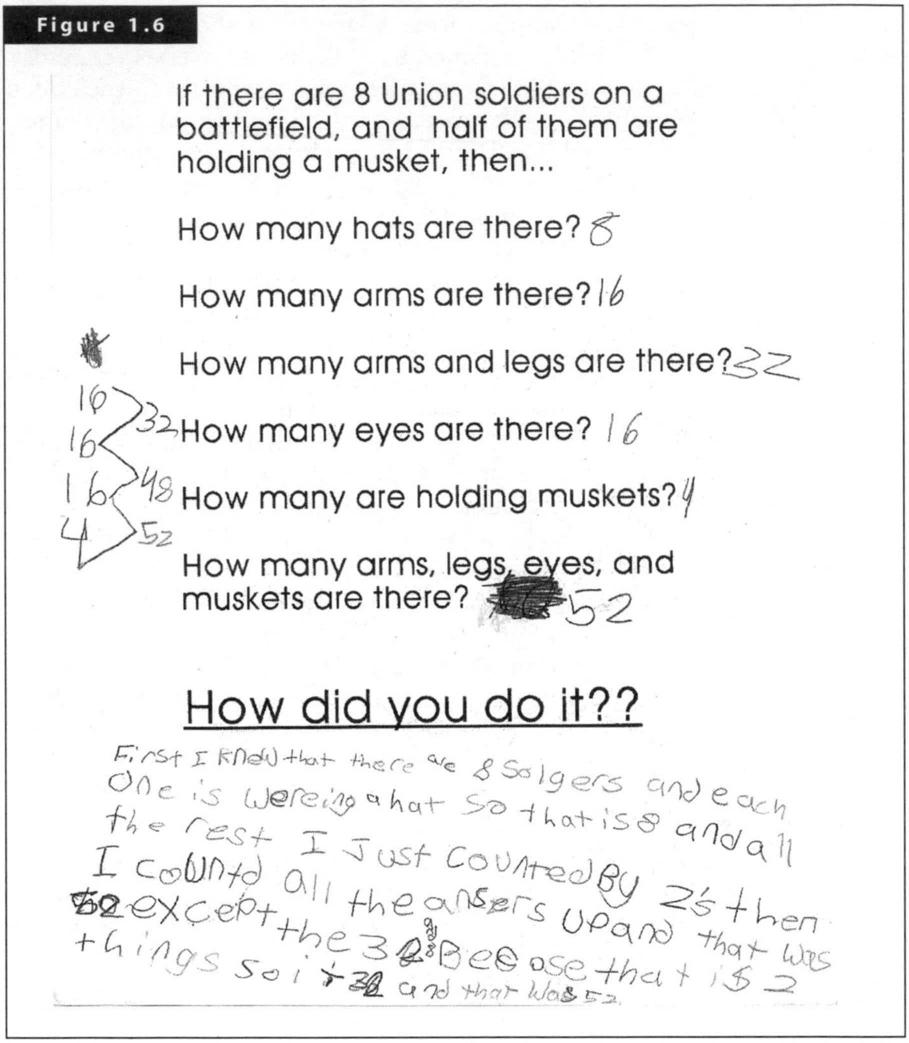

If there are 8 Union soldiers on a battlefield, and half of them are holding a musket, then...

How many hats are there? 8

How many arms are there? 16

How many arms and legs are there? 32

How many eyes are there? 16

How many are holding muskets? 4

How many arms, legs, eyes, and muskets are there? 52

16 ⟩ 32
16 ⟨
16 ⟩ 48
4 ⟩ 52

How did you do it??

First I knew that there are 8 solgers and each one is wereing a hat so that is 8 and all the rest I just counted by 2's then I counted all the ansers up and that was 52 except the 32 Becose that is 2 things so i + 32 and that was 52.

"Yes, I can!" Carly jumped in. "Here, look, Jack. Take tens strips; if you take five of them, see how many strips you have? It's just the same number, right?"

"Yeah," said Jack, watching Carly intently.

"Well, if I put four units next to it, what's the answer?" she asked.

"54?"

"Yep! Good, Jack. Now what if I put four tens strips down?" She continued to question him without using the strips. He soon understood what she was saying. Not that Jack could now add double-digit numbers, but he had a visual model to refer to, from Carly's explanation.

Sometimes the explanations are hard for the kids to understand. Dave shared his solution to the following problem:

> Flour at the General Store costs 5 cents a pound. Potatoes cost 3 cents a pound. Cloth costs 10 cents a yard. Licorice costs 2 cents apiece.
>
> You need to buy 4 pounds of flour, 3 pounds of potatoes, 5 yards of cloth, and four pieces of licorice.
>
> How much money did you spend?
>
> How did you do it?

"I added 10 up five times, so that's 50," said Dave, "then added 5 four times, that was 70, then added 3 three times, and it was 79, then 2 four times, and it was 87."

"OK," I said with a heavy sigh. "Who could follow that?" A few hands went up. "Dave, do you want to go through that again, or does someone else want to try to explain it a bit slower?" I left the decision up to Dave.

"I will, Jill," said Kyle.

"Go for it," said Dave.

"Well, what I did was this. I used unifix cubes. I took out how many I needed for each thing. Like, I needed 5 yards of cloth, and cloth cost 10 cents, so I got out 50 unifix cubes. Then I did that for all of them and added it up."

"Why don't you go ahead and do that, Kyle," I asked. I wanted all the kids to see him actually solving the problem as he had done. He went to get out all the unifix cubes he needed. He had them all in front of him.

"Then I needed to add them all up. I knew that it would take a long time to just count them up so I put them into groups of ten." He proceeded to put the pile of unifix cubes in front of him into groups of ten.

"Then it was easy for me to count by tens. And there were seven cubes left, so I got 87 too, like Dave," was Kyle's explanation.

It was important that I ask Kyle to continue through the whole problem. It gave some of the inexperienced mathematicians a chance to see how Kyle grouped the pile. By sitting in a circle or on our platform, all the kids could watch what Kyle was doing. That step had been left out of his written explanation and his verbal sharing. It was also important to let Dave share his equation the way he did. Just because I can't follow numbers that quickly doesn't mean other kids can't. Jacob, for instance, could follow Dave's explanation perfectly. He adds in the same quick way. All kids need to share and be questioned if there is a part of the explanation that is unclear.

One problem Aisha had written for the kids that I remember having a long discussion about went like this: "Six people want to share these five pies. What fraction of a pie do they each get?"

"I just cut each one into sixths, so each of them got 5/6," said fourth grader Caitlin. Chris's solution was to cut them all in half and keep the extras! Sixth grader Kim said, "First I cut three of them in half, and then the other two I cut in thirds. So, I added 1/3 and 1/2 and got 5/6."

"That's just what I did too," said Megan.

But it was more difficult for me to visualize fifth grader Carly's solution: "I divided the pieces into thirds and gave each person 2/3. Then I added the 1/6 and 2/3, that was 10/12. Then I divided 10 and 12 by 2, and I got 5/6."

"Huh? Wait, Carly, I don't understand what you did. Does anyone else? Can you do it up on the whiteboard and let us follow along?" I asked. She proceeded to draw six stick figures. She then drew five circles to represent the pies. She cut four pies into thirds and showed how each of the six stick figures could get 2/3. Then she divided the last circle into sixths, and added 2/3 and 1/6. She converted the 2/3 to 8/12, and the 1/6 to 2/12, and added them to get 10/12. Then she reduced 10/12 to be 5/6.

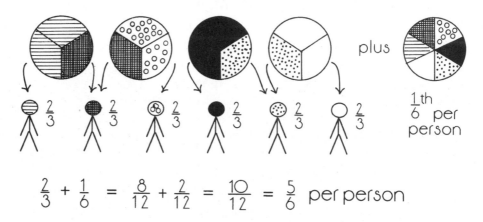

$$\frac{2}{3} + \frac{1}{6} = \frac{8}{12} + \frac{2}{12} = \frac{10}{12} = \frac{5}{6} \text{ per person}$$

"Oh, I get it. See how she just cut it into thirds and then there was a whole pie left over. I get it," said Kyle.

"I'm glad you do. Why did you cut it into thirds?" I asked. For some reason, I just couldn't see what she had done.

"I don't know. It just looked like I had enough," she said.

"Is that why you divided yours in half first, Kim?"

"Yeah, it was easy to start with half."

"Wow. Well, Caitlin, I did it your way. I just cut the pies into sixths," I said. Through this sharing of methods, I learned how differently children first think about a problem. I looked at how much Carly knew about fractions to be able to solve that problem the way she did, how comfortable with fractions Kim and Megan were to approach the problem the way they did. I would have assumed the easiest way to do that problem would be to do what Caitlin and I did. It reaffirmed my belief that kids need to be able to solve problems independently without always first being told how to use formulas and rules.

Explain Your Thinking

I think the reason we write about problems is so that Jill, as well as the students, understand how we do them. And we understand them better ourselves. I think it's important to do it. To understand how we did it. And it works too, because I never had to write about how I solved problems until I got in this class, and I never had really thought about it. It's helped me a lot. Now I understand how I'm doing it instead of the teacher explaining how to do it and then we do it. And when the class shares, it's cool because you learn different ways to solve stuff.

Kim, age 12

The biggest choice we have is the choice of learning how we want to. Like when we have math. Some people use cubes, and some people use their heads. But if we did math sheets, Jill wouldn't know how we learn.

Laura and Rachel, age 9

We don't just write the answer because then it doesn't tell us what we did. Jill wouldn't know what we did. Neither would anyone else. We need to write about how we solved problems 'cause it's more important to know how we did. Not just the answer.

Jacob, age 7

Allowing children to create algorithms and solve problems independently, and giving them time to share their strategies with the whole class, are important. Children also need to show their thinking in writing. I ask my students to explain every problem they solve either orally or in writing. I remember when my third graders were taking one of the standardized tests that all children in our public school system take. I asked them to tell me about their experience with taking the math section of the test.

"It was easy!"

"I thought it was dumb."

"How come we didn't have to explain how we got our answers?"

That last was my favorite response.

What can you learn about a child's mathematical thinking process by just looking at the answer? Nothing. Standardized tests don't care about thinking process; they only care about right answers. I'm thrilled that my children understand the importance of that step of solving a problem.

During a phone conversation I had with Kyle, he was telling me about his new fifth-grade class. He told me he had a great story to tell me about math. I was intrigued.

"Well, while we were doing minute math . . . ," he began.

"What's minute math?" I asked.

"Well, it's where our teacher gives us a bunch of equations and we have to see how many we can do in a minute."

"Oh."

"Well, in the middle of it, it was really quiet, and I raised my hand. My teacher said, 'Yes Kyle?' and I said, 'You know, minute math doesn't show you any of our real math skills.'"

I wanted to cry. "Yes, Kyle! You get it! So what did your teacher say to you?"

"Well, he said that we'd be going over them afterwards."

"So what did you do afterwards?" I asked.

"He just told us the answers. We never write about how we solve problems really." Kyle knows so much about the importance of becoming a mathematician.

I get vital information from students' written explanations. I learn how they are thinking, what strategies they are using, and how they approach a problem. Children use detailed pictures, drawings, manipulatives, or written numbers to solve problems. Some children use a combination of all these strategies, some usually stick with one, and some go from one strategy to another in progression. (For more on this, see my chapter called "Beyond Answers," in *New Entries*, edited by Ruth Hubbard and Karen Ernst.) By having my children describe what strategies they have used to solve a problem, I am able to learn more about them as mathematicians. I see such a rich variety in learning strategies in just one problem the children solve.

The following problem was written because I wanted to see the different approaches my students had to division and remainders. (This problem was written when we were studying the 1940s. We learned that M&M's were invented in order for the soldiers to have candy on the front line. The slogan "Melts in your mouth not in your hand" was because of that.)

■ M&M Problem

There are six soldiers in the field. One of them pulls out a package of M&M's. There are 47 M&M's in the package.

How many M&M's does each soldier get? Are there any extras? What do they do with them?

How did you solve this?

First grader Kimberly's written explanation of how she solved this problem was, "I got six unifix cubes for the soldiers and 47 for the M&M's and counted them up" (Figure 1.7). Had I only asked Kimberly to write the answer (with no explanation), I wouldn't have known how she came to her answer. She put six cubes out in a row for the soldiers. Then she counted out 47 other cubes and shared them out between the six soldier cubes. There were five extra cubes.

Shanti also used the sharing method of division, but she used drawings instead. She wrote, "I put six circles out and 47 lines out. And I drew lines from one line to a circle until there was not enough and that was how I got 7 R5" (Figure 1.8).

Caitlin used the fraction model of division. She knew that each soldier could get seven, and she then divided the rest into sixths. Her written answer was 7 5/6.

Figure 1.7

There are 6 soldiers in the field. One of them pulls out a package of M & M's. There are 47 M & M's in the package.

How many M & M's do each soldier get? 7

Are there any extra's? 2 extras

What do they do with them? eat them

HOW DID YOU SOLVE THIS? I got 21x2

I wanna fix cuods. for the Soldiers
and 47 for the mahdms ano crit
them U9

Figure 1.8

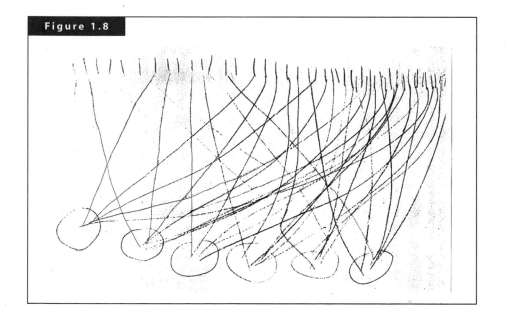

From the children's written responses, it becomes apparent if more questioning is needed. For the M&M problem, Ross wrote as his explanation, 47 ÷ 6. His answer said 7 R5, yet for the question, Are there any extras? Ross wrote no. I asked him to write how he did 47 divided by 6. He brought his paper back to me, and he had written, "I took 6 cubes and 47 cubes and went one for you, one for you, and on like that." Obviously, Ross knew the symbol for division, probably from Calendar (see Chapter 3), but he didn't know how to solve the problem without some sort of manipulative.

With the school desk problem, also written during our 1940s study, Megan wrote for her solution, "I did 28 × 4 = 112. I did it in the grouping" (Figure 1.9). Megan groups numbers when she multiplies and adds.

Many times, the written explanation confuses me, and I rely on the drawing to help. Chelsea wrote, "I drew four groups out of 28 and counted by 4's and got 112." Her drawing showed 28 groups of 4, not 4 *out of* 28. It was clear to me that Chelsea needed help with the language of math when describing solutions.

Written explanations are an easy way to check to see if kids know what they are doing. It's easy to look at someone else's paper and jot down an answer, especially if one is not asked to explain the solution. I used to do that all the time as a child. I can't believe I made it through fractions in elementary school. All I did was copy my friends' answers. If I had had to explain even one of my solutions, I would have been caught. Maybe, though, instead of my then getting into trouble, my teacher would have been able to help me. That is what I am able to do when my students bring me a problem that they clearly don't understand.

Figure 1.9

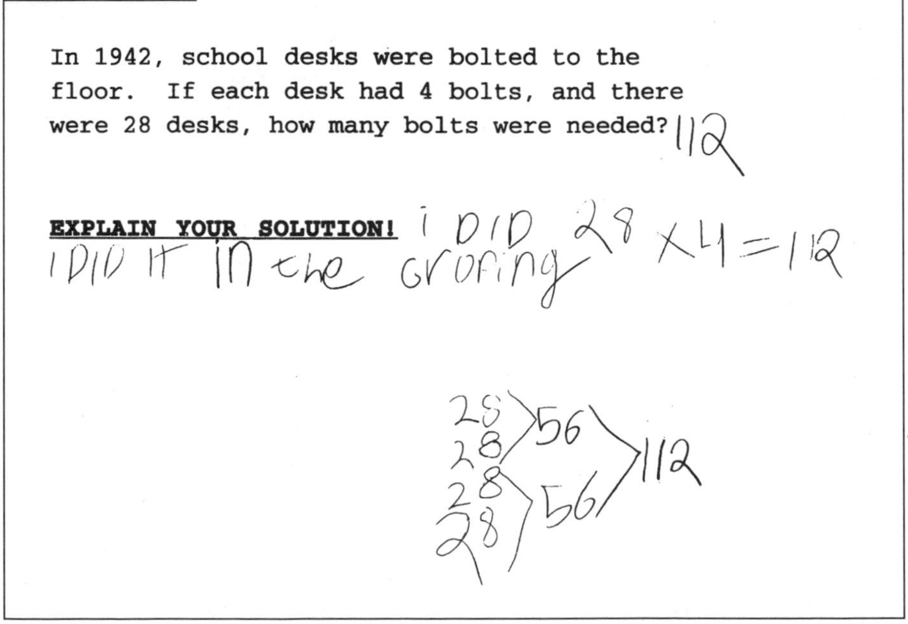

In 1942, school desks were bolted to the floor. If each desk had 4 bolts, and there were 28 desks, how many bolts were needed? 112

EXPLAIN YOUR SOLUTION! i DID 28 × 8 = 112
I DID IT IN the groping

Kathryn was a first grader when she solved the following problem:

> You have one dogsled with 15 dogs. You meet up with another team of people that also has a dogsled with 15 dogs. How many dogs are there now altogether?
>
> Then two more teams show up, each with 15 dogs.
>
> Now how many dogs are there?
>
> Explain how you solved this problem.

Her solution was not written anywhere on the paper, but she had an explanation. It read, "I counted numbers and the number stopped at 15, and it was all the way to 15 + 15." I looked at her drawing and saw rows and rows of numbers written 1 through 15. I knew I would need to have a conference with her.

"Kathryn, can you tell me how you did this?"

"Uh, well, I didn't really get it," she said.

"OK, let's see what you have. Can you explain why you have all of these rows of 15?"

"Well, I'm not sure."

"Why don't we read the problem again, and maybe you'll remember," I said. She followed along as I read her the problem.

"Oh, yeah, well I did the top part first. I wanted to do 15 and another 15, but I got lost."

"That's good, Kathryn. How did you know that you wanted to do 15 and another 15?"

"Because it said that there were 15 and then 15 more came, so I figured it was 15 and another 15," she said.

"That's great that you knew that, Kathryn. OK, so how do you think you could do 15 and 15 more?"

"Well, I could go use unifix cubes maybe." And off she went to solve the top part of the problem. That's what she could do. Because I aim to appropriately challenge each child in my class, I assume that there will be some kids who will be able to do just parts of problems, and that's fine. When we shared as a class, Kathryn was able to see the next steps of the problem.

Some children solved the dogsled problem by computing the numbers in their head.

Dave's solution read, "First, I knew that 15 + 15 = 30. So I added 10, which is 40, then 5 to finish off the first 15. Then I had 45. So I added 10, and that was 55. Then I added 5 to finish off the 15, and 5 more to 55 is 60, so 60 is the answer."

Carly's solution was, "Two dogsleds with 15 dogs meet up together, and I know that 15 + 15 = 30. Then two more dogsleds meet together, so I did 30 + 30 = 60. I did it in my head."

Kyle wrote, "Well, I took six 10's and that was 60. Why I took six 10's is because I just took away the 5's and four 10's was 40, and four 5's was 20, I added that to 40, and it was 60. I used my brain."

Differences in computation techniques come out so clearly through the kids' writing. We might expect that by fifth grade most kids are using the same strategies, but that is not the case. Older children need to be able to solve problems in their own different ways as well. Following are a few different solutions to this problem:

> There are 12 brothers and 13 sisters in a family. If no more than two children can share a room, and sisters and brothers do not sleep in the same room, how many bedrooms does their house have?

Ten-year-old Carly wrote, "I grouped all of them and then added the rooms."

Nine-year-old Megan wrote, "I counted by 2's until I got to 12, and then I counted how many times, and that was 6. There were six 2's in 13 and an extra, so there's 13."

Twelve-year-old Kim wrote, "13. $12 \div 2 = 6$ and $13 \div 2 = 6\ 1/2$. Since there can't be a half, we just add an extra room."

Eleven-year-old Cory wrote, "13 rooms. I divided 12 by 2 and got 6. And divided 13 by 2 and got 6 1/2. And then I added $6 + 6 + 1$ and got 13 rooms."

Communication either orally or in writing is the way I learn how children approach computation. Just because my kids don't do pages of worksheets doesn't mean they aren't computing.

When kids write about their solutions, it almost forces them to rethink a problem they have already solved. It reinforces understanding of their solution. The written explanations also serve as a reminder for kids as to how they solved a problem. As they look through their math portfolios, students don't have to figure out how they solved a problem; the writing is there to remind them.

Building a foundation for a mathematician isn't hard. It's actually easier than following a strict curriculum. The foundation is all about listening to your students, respecting their learning processes, and learning as much as you can about them by observing their strategies. Building a mathematical foundation for your students is not just about your students, though; it's also about you.

Have clear goals as to what you are trying to teach. What and why are you teaching what you are teaching?

Have a wide and solid foundation in math and problem solving for yourself. If you are trying to teach fractions, do you understand fractions yourself?

Have a good idea of where your children are coming from and where they are in their mathematical development. Is what you are presenting to them appropriate for each child?

Question what you give your students to do, observe how they are responding to what you give them, notice all the strategies they are using, and use what you are learning about your students to stretch and challenge yourself as teacher. Go beyond the curriculum guides, and create mathematical experiences for your students using what you have learned from them.

2

What's Your Problem?

My students have been the ones to teach me about mathematical development. That's not to say I haven't learned from mathematical curricula as well. *Opening Eyes to Mathematics* (Arcidiacono, Head, and Pollett 1995) and *Visual Mathematics* (Bennett and Foreman 1995) have been very influential in my growth as an educator. *Math Excursions* (Burk, Snider, and Symonds 1991) and *Posing and Solving Problems with Story Boxes* (Snider and Burk 1994) have also been useful. Yet, by observing my students over the years, listening to what they were saying, and respecting their learning, I discovered that using only one curriculum was not going to work in my classroom. I learned I could draw upon different curricula for certain lessons and still create learning situations for my students. For instance, the *Opening Eyes* curriculum was written more or less for grades 2 and 3, yet many of the ideas were appropriate for sixth graders as well. *Visual Mathematics* was written for older students, yet I have used some of the ideas from that curriculum with first graders.

Over the years of pulling activities from different curricula, I have realized that the most important aspect of my math program is not necessarily *which* program I use. The most important aspect of my math program is to give my students as much exposure as I can to all aspects of the mathematical continuum. So I make sure to give them a balance of concepts and ideas throughout the year. It is also important that my problems include the 13 NCTM Standards (in this book, I refer to the 13 NCTM Standards written for grades K–4: please see page 147 for information on the 13 NCTM Standards for grades 5–8):

NCTM Standards for K–4

1. Mathematics as Problem Solving
2. Mathematics as Communication
3. Mathematics as Reasoning

4. Mathematical Connections
5. Estimation
6. Number Sense and Numeration
7. Concepts of Whole Number Operations
8. Whole Number Computation
9. Geometry and Spatial Sense
10. Measurement
11. Statistics and Probability
12. Fractions and Decimals
13. Patterns and Relationships

The problems I write incorporate a variety of these standards throughout the week, month, and year. I write different types of problems depending on what concepts we are studying and what I want to learn from my students. For instance, one day they might be solving a problem that focuses on division, and the next day a problem focusing on measurement. The focus of the concept changes often, as does the type of problem I write. It's hard to avoid falling into the trap of overteaching computation. I do my best to keep a good balance between the standards and the curriculum guidelines required by my school district.

For purposes of explanation, I have classified the types of problems I write into the following five categories:

- Raw
- Topic-connected
- Multistep
- Open-ended
- Kid-written

Sometimes a problem fits into more than one category.

Raw Problems

I suppose you could call this kind of problem computation. I like the term *raw problem* better. (An example of a raw problem would be an equation such as $46 + 39$.) Computation to me means page after page of sums—something I don't give my kids.

The kids get a lot of practice with raw problems during Calendar (see Chapter 3). As they do the "ways to make" section of Calendar, they are writing and solving equations. I also give them raw problems to solve during math workshop. For instance, I ask them to write as many equations as they can for a given number (see Dave's variations on the number 80 in Figure 2.1). There several reasons why I like this simple problem so much:

- I can give it over and over again throughout the year; I just change the numbers.

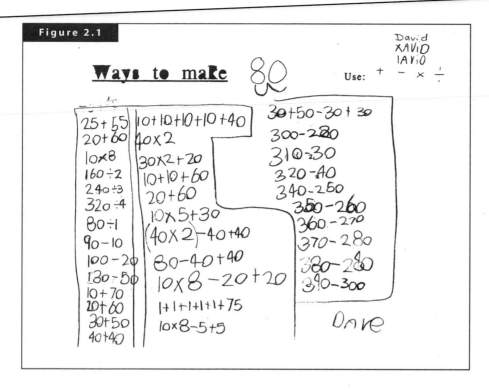

Figure 2.1

- I can easily assign different numbers to each child in the class so they are all working at their own developmental levels of understanding.
- The kids are getting computation practice, but they are in control of how much they do and how much they challenge themselves. The more operations they use, the more equations they do, the more they show me how able and willing they are to challenge themselves independently. If I just handed them a sheet full of equations to compute, they wouldn't be challenging themselves; they would be doing what I gave them.

Often the kids are asked to describe exactly how they solved a raw problem. Sixth grader Kim chose to solve 1 1/2 ÷ 2/3. She drew a model and wrote in detail how she solved the equation (Figure 2.2).

The year I taught a combined class of fourth, fifth, and sixth graders, the kids did 15 minutes of raw problems before math workshop every morning. Aisha or I would write a few equations on the whiteboard, and the kids worked on these. Some of the equations were just raw problems, others were short word problems. Sometimes we would ask the kids to solve them in their heads and then write down what their strategies were. During the 15 minutes, the kids worked at their own pace to do as many as they could. One morning Kyle solved two of the four equations on the board. He wrote how he had solved them in his head: "For 58 − 46 I just added 12 to 46, and that was 58, so it must be 12. For 463 + 939 I first added 900 and 400 and then added the 39 and then the 63."

Figure 2.2

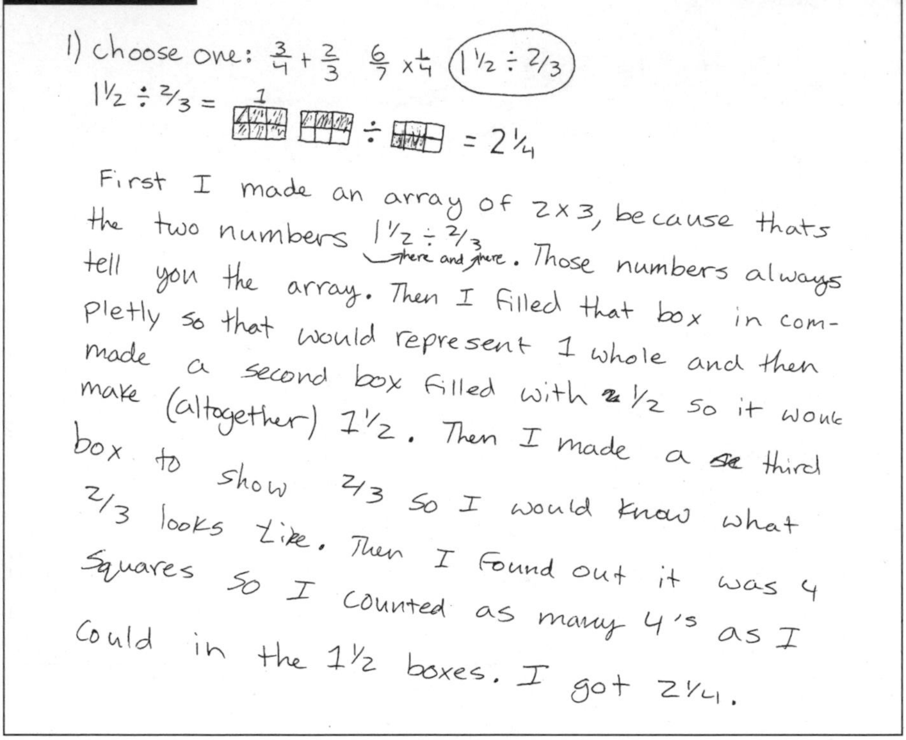

> 1) choose one: $\frac{3}{4} + \frac{2}{3}$ $\frac{6}{7} \times \frac{1}{4}$ $\left(1\frac{1}{2} \div \frac{2}{3}\right)$
>
> $1\frac{1}{2} \div \frac{2}{3} = $ ... $= 2\frac{1}{4}$
>
> First I made an array of 2x3, because thats the two numbers $1\frac{1}{2} \div \frac{2}{3}$ there and there. Those numbers always tell you the array. Then I filled that box in completly so that would represent 1 whole and then made a second box filled with 2½ so it would make (altogether) 1½. Then I made a third box to show ⅔ so I would know what ⅔ looks like. Then I found out it was 4 squares so I counted as many 4's as I could in the 1½ boxes. I got 2¼.

Topic-Connected Problems

These are problems I write that have to do with what we are studying at that time. I think it's important to make connections between the various subjects we are teaching. I try not to write topic-connected problems just for the sake of integrating but rather to teach something new as well, or to reinforce something we have already learned.

Many problems written during our 1940s study had to do with the home front, Victory Gardens, ration books, Europe, and the war.

During our Arctic study, the problems used vocabulary such as *mukluk, kayak, umiak,* and the names of Arctic peoples:

■ Arctic Store Problem

At the store there are these items at these prices:

Parka	$35
Mukluk	$40
Pair of warm gloves	$25
Book	$ 4
Toothpaste	$ 1.50

Toothbrush	$ 0.75
Crackers and cheese	$10.25

You have $75 to spend at the Arctic Store. Write down what you bought, how much money you spent, and how much money you have left.

Make your sheet neat. Explain how you solved this problem.

We were learning about the beaded necklaces made by Inuit woman. After some children completed the following problem, they used the rest of math workshop time to create some necklaces using native North American pattern ideas.

■ Arctic People Problem

There were five Inuit beadmakers who each beaded six necklaces. They put all of their necklaces together and gave them away equally to three women.

Two of the women gave away four of their necklaces, and the other woman gave away three.

How many necklaces did each woman have left?

How many necklaces did the women have altogether now?

Show and explain how you got your answers.

Most of the problems the kids solve at the beginning of math workshop are topic-connected problems that usually take just one workshop to complete. But other topic-connected problems are multistep problems.

Multistep Problems

Multistep problems are those that require more than one solution or more than one step to complete. The kids go as far as they can with the problem. They stop at the place they are challenged beyond what they can do.

Following is an example of a multistep problem from the class of fourth, fifth, and sixth graders that was written during the time we were harvesting walnuts to sell. (A friend and colleague, Bob Carlson, lived on property in town that had a walnut orchard. We asked if we could harvest the nuts and sell them. We walked down to the orchard several times during the fall. We raised over $200.)

Notice that the walnut problem, like the Ellis Island problem that follows, doesn't ask many specific questions. I write statements, and the kids are asked to think about what the questions could be. I learned this from the *Visual Mathematics* (Bennett and Foreman 1995) curriculum. In that curriculum there are many lessons that focus on pulling questions from situations. I took what I had learned and wrote statements that I could try with my students. It is up to the child to pose the questions, to figure out what could be asked from the statements written. This pulling questions from statements helps kids deal with problems in their daily lives. For example, you need gas, but you have less than 1/4 tank left. You don't know where the next station is, and you have 60 miles left to drive. You only have $10. The questions aren't cut-and-dried. There are many things to consider and a variety of circumstances. What I might choose to do might be different from what you would choose to do. I think it's important to let kids learn how to ask the questions, to figure out what is being asked without always telling them, and to let them explain why and how they came up with the questions they decided to solve.

■ Walnut Problem

A class of 26 children harvested walnuts. Each child harvested 4 pounds of nuts.

Half (1/2) the kids sold all their walnuts. They sold them for $4.50 a pound.

Seven kids sold only 2 pounds of walnuts each, but they sold them for $5 a pound.

Six kids sold only 1 pound of walnuts each, but they sold them for $3.50 a pound.

The kids put all the money they made into the bank. They made 5 percent interest on their money each month. At the end of four months, they took their money out of the bank.

They decided to spend their money on a field trip. They couldn't decide where to go—the mountains or the beach—so they flipped a coin. What were the chances of the coin's landing on heads?

They decided to go to the mountains. They were 65 miles away, and they figured out that they needed 8 gallons of gas. Gas cost $1.35 a gallon. They got 9 gallons of gas.

They reached the mountain and spent 1/2 their remaining money on food.

On the way home, they found a shortcut that cut their travel time in half, but the number of miles was the same. How could that be?

They had no more money to spend, so they decided to sell the rest of the walnuts that their classmates hadn't sold. They sold all the remaining walnuts for $3.50.

Each part of the problem feeds off the previous question. Many of the kids didn't know what percentage meant, so that was a good assessment opportunity for me.

These problems are fun to discuss because there are usually many different answers—anything from computation discrepancies to creative choices.

During the time we were studying the 1900s, we were collecting stories about how our ancestors came to America. We had learned about Ellis

Island and had found it intriguing. We watched a PBS special on Ellis Island, and the kids found out if they had relatives that had come through Ellis Island. Much of what we were learning about I incorporated into the following problem:

■ **Trip to Ellis Island**

You have decided to leave your homeland and go to America. Your homeland is in Eastern Europe.

1997 will be 89 years from now.

You can't take all your belongings. You have filled 2/3 of a suitcase with your things. You have a brother, a sister, and your mother going with you. Your sister's suitcase is 2/5 filled, your brother's suitcase is 1/4 filled, and your mother's suitcase is totally filled. You put all the things from those suitcases together to save space.

The shipping company is requiring you to stay overnight at the shipping hotel. There are 63 other people at the hotel waiting to go to America on the ship. One-quarter (1/4) of those people are going to stay in New York, 2/3 are going to Chicago, and the rest are headed to Boston.

Once on the boat, you are directed to go to the steerage class. Half (1/2) the passengers are not in the steerage class. Of those people not in steerage class, 2/5 go up to first class. The rest of them are in second class. The other 1/2 of the passengers are in steerage class with you and your family.

The trip is hard, but you finally spot the Statue of Liberty in the harbor. You look around and notice that one out of every three people is crying at the sight of the statue.

Once in line, you see people getting checked by a medical inspector. Your mother looks at you and notices redness in your eye. What should she do? You have a decision to make. Make your decision and write what happened to you. Did you get to go through the gates, or do you get shipped back to your homeland? Write about what happened to you.

Since the kids were pulling questions from the written statements, many of the solutions were different depending on their perceptions of the problem. For instance, twelve-year-old Kim said she did not merge the mother's things with the children's things. She said the mother would have had more items to take with her, so only the children merged their possessions.

Concerning the number of people crying because of the Statue of Liberty, Aaron thought it was 1/3 of his own family, while others thought it was 1/3 of all the passengers.

Kids had several different ideas for the last step of this problem. Alex wrote, "My mother sprinkled baby powder in my eye. It raised some suspicion among the inspectors, but they let me through." Carly wrote, "My mom puts me in a potato bag and carries me with her until she gets past the inspectors. I get through the gates." Cory wrote, "'My God, you do have a redness in your eye!' my mother exclaimed. Quickly, she revealed a pirate's patch. 'I was prepared for this,' she said quietly. I put the patch over the eye and when it was my turn I said, 'I lost the eye by a stick.' I thought he wouldn't believe me, but the next thing I knew we were at the kissing post!"

Questions like these are fun to put into a problem. They make for interesting discussions, since everyone has a different idea of what happened to them. Plus, it gives the kids a chance to put what they have learned into their work. I like to use problems like this. It takes away some of the "Is it right?" phobia. How can opinions and ideas be wrong? I also want my students to know that problems aren't only related to math. Problems are to be solved. Sometimes that involves math, and sometimes that involves language, social situations, and other things.

I have also used topic-connected multistep problems with my first/third-grade classes. When we were building a time travel machine in our classroom the year we were time travelers, I wrote the following problem and the kids worked on it as partners:

■ Time Travel Machine

You are going to design one wall of a time travel machine.

The wall should measure 25 square units.

You should have 12 buttons on the wall: 1/3 of the buttons should be purple; 1/3 of the buttons should be green; and 1/3 of the buttons should be yellow. Label the buttons, and tell what they do.

You will need a window that is smaller than 15 square units but larger then 10 square units.

You will need a sign inside the machine that tells where and when you are. The sign should be less than 1/2 the size of the window.

Name your machine. Write a short story about it.

During our study of the 1940s the kids worked one math workshop on the Victory Garden problem. The concepts addressed in this problem are multiplication, addition, and area. I was planning a long problem on area that the kids would begin soon, so I wanted to give them more practice with area.

■ Victory Garden Problem

You are going to plant a Victory Garden. The vegetables you plant will be carrots, lettuce, tomatoes, red peppers, and zucchini; and the flowers you plant will be sunflowers and marigolds.

You want to have more tomato plants than all other vegetables.

You want to plant three times as many carrots as zucchini.

You want to plant twice as many lettuce plants as red pepper plants.

You want to plant sunflowers on one side of the garden and marigolds all around the border of the garden.

> You have an area of land that is 6 × 8 square feet. Use graph paper and make one square be one square foot of land. What will your garden look like?

The kids worked as partners and created very different gardens.

Whenever there was a question about a specific part of a problem, we met as a group to discuss it. Not all of my youngest students knew what it meant to have three times as many of something, as it asks in the Victory Garden problem, so we would share ideas.

Kyle said that he had multiplied by 3. Melissa, who is a very inexperienced mathematician, said she got out five unifix cubes and put them together in a strip. "Then I knew that three more would need three more, so I got out three more," she added. What she had actually done was to put three more unifix cubes on top of her five.

"Does anyone have any comments for Melissa?" I asked.

"I think she put three more, not three times as many," Megan said. And Megan explained to Melissa how she could get out two more strips of five unifix cubes. Melissa was then able to show twice as many, though she still didn't internalize the notion of "times as much."

Open-Ended Problems

Many districts are incorporating open-ended problems into their curricula. The state of Oregon tests students using an open-ended problem. But I wonder about some of those open-ended problems. If the problem requires a specific answer, how can it be open-ended? Someone once told me that an open-ended problem means that the child has to solve the problem in more than one way and explain the thinking, but that is what kids should be doing with *every* problem.

To me, an open-ended problem is one for which there are many possible solutions—a problem for which children all have different solutions and need to explain them to the class.

Many problems I give my students have to do with exploration. For instance, I might ask them to explore the pattern blocks, write down what they did, and be prepared to share. These are wonderful types of problems, or explorations, because there are as many answers as students in the class.

For one particular exploration, Kyle decided to explore the sides of the pattern blocks (Figure 2.3).

I remember Dave exploring the angles of the pattern blocks. He discovered all the angle measurements of each block by knowing that the corner of a square has a 90° angle. "Well, I knew that the square has 90° angles, so I put the other blocks on top of the square. Like, the skinny white diamond is 30°, since you can put three diamonds into the angle of the square" (Figure 2.4).

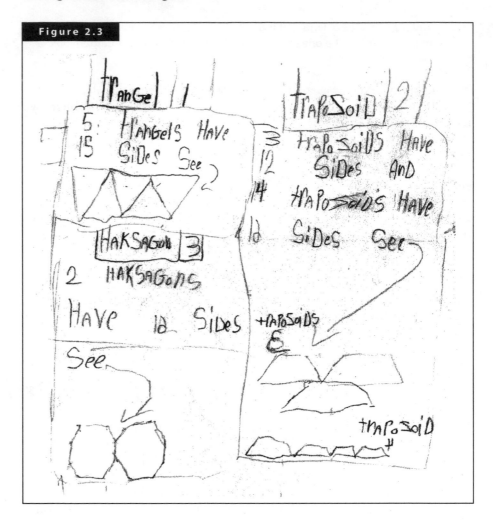

Figure 2.3

Another exploration I gave one day was simply to measure things around the room. I told the kids they could not use a ruler.

"Then how are we supposed to measure anything?" asked Megan.

"Good question. How can you measure something without a ruler or a standard unit like that?" I asked the group.

"Well, you could make your hand be the unit maybe," shared Kyle.

"Or maybe graph paper pieces?" Dave said.

"What about unifix cubes? Wouldn't that work?" asked Tessia.

And off they went to create a unit of measure and use it to measure different objects around the room (Figure 2.5). We all learned so much about standard and nonstandard measurements from these discoveries.

Another type of open-ended problem is one where I begin the sentence and the kids have to figure out what to do next. For instance, during one math workshop the kids were given the following sentence starter: "If one

Figure 2.4

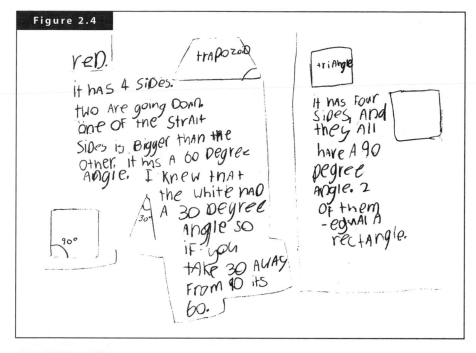

Figure 2.5

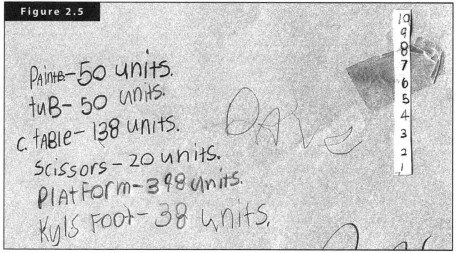

hexagon has six sides, then . . ." Many ideas emerged from that simple inquiry. Kyle worked on fractions and sides, and even drew a cartoon (Figure 2.6).

Here are some open-ended problems I have given my kids to work on during math workshop. These investigations could be used at any grade level. The investigation would be the same, but the solutions would be quite different.

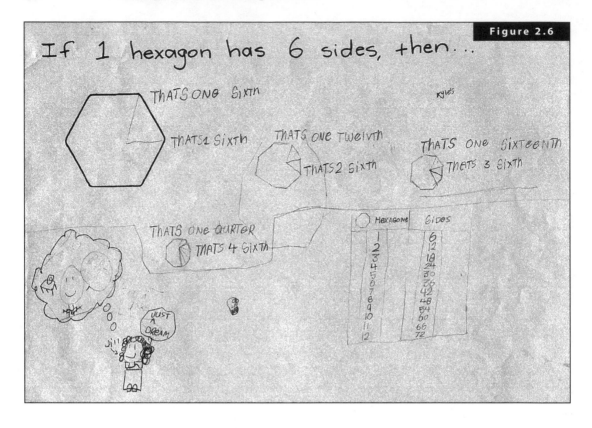

Figure 2.6

- Do more from Calendar: more ways to make, more fractions.
- What can you do with the number 10?
- Investigate patterns around the room.
- Measure things using a ruler, a yardstick, a meter stick, or unifix cubes.
- Investigate the geoboards.
- Make up a game using pattern blocks.
- How would you teach someone how to do addition (or subtraction, multiplication, division, or fractions)?
- Do anything that is challenging for you.
- Write yourself a problem and see how many different ways you can solve it.
- Create patterns that would make attractive tiles in a house.
- Calculate the area and perimeter of objects around the room. Explain how you measured the area and perimeter if the object was not a square or a rectangle.

I also write open-ended problems that seem a bit more structured yet still can have many different outcomes. I always hated filling out book order forms. You know the ones—the kids fill out forms for the books they want and bring in the forms and their checks, and then we have to calculate the amounts. I don't know about you, but my totals never came out right. I always had either too much money or not enough. (Finally, I just asked a parent to do this job!) I wrote my own problem for the kids to do using an old book order form:

> You need to order five different books. Write the names of the books you ordered, the price of each book, and how much you spent altogether.
>
> When you finish, explain how you solved this problem.

The kids were allowed to buy whatever books they wanted. It was interesting to see the younger kids work on this problem. Chris wrote, "I started doing the prices. I used cubes, and I ended up with $20.40." He made a chart to keep track of his books (Figure 2.7).

Another type of open-ended problem I like to write is one where the kids are asked to create a theory or formula. My fourth, fifth, and sixth graders were working on circumference. There was a huge fallen Douglas fir tree in the woods behind the school. We asked a friend and a parent to cut the tree into 30 parts so we could have a meeting circle in the clearing in the woods. We made our circle; each child had a stump to sit on. I wrote several problems that focused on the stumps, to which circumference lent itself very well.

I read them a story called *The Librarian Who Measured the Earth*, by Kathryn Lasky. It is about Eratosthenes and how he figured out how to

Figure 2.7

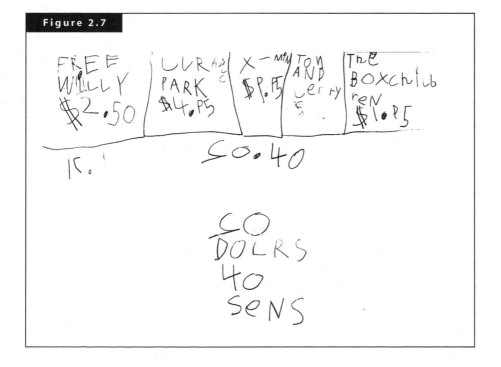

measure the circumference of the earth using shadows formed by the sun. We had learned that even though there was already a formula for measuring circumference, Eratosthenes wanted to do something else. From the information we learned, I wrote the following problem for my students:

■ Creating Circumference

Eratosthenes figured out how to measure the circumference of the earth. There was a formula for measuring circumference even then, but he made up his own way.

Figure out a way that is different than the way you know, to measure the circumference of the red circle. You can do it any way you want, but you can't use pi or a string.

Be creative!

When you have finished, write your theory down.

Answer these questions:

Will your theory work on other circles? Why, or why not?

Will your theory work on spheres? Why, or why not?

The kids invented several ways to figure out circumference. Betsy figured it out using different shapes inside the circle: "I made a square in the middle of the circle. And then made a cross. In the square, the cross made four triangles, and I measured one of the triangles and got 2.0. Assuming the rest were 2.0, I quickly added them up, which equaled 8.0. The rest was not in the square. I measured going to the biggest point and measuring from the middle of the outside of the square. It added up to .5. Then I added all of it up, which equaled 10."

I thought Kim's method was particularly interesting. She took one of her jelly beans and used that as a unit of measure. Her written solution was, "Take the circle and split it in fourths, drawing lines to show the fourths. Take one jelley belley, which = 1/2 inch, then measure one-fourth of the circle with the jelley belley. Add all the half inches together and times that by 4." She also came up with a formula: "Operation: $(1/2 \times N) \times 4 = x$." At the end, we discussed which was the most accurate theory and which was the quickest way of measuring the circle.

Kid-Written Problems

Another type of problem is written by the kids themselves. Having kids create their own problems is an important part of their mathematical development. It helps them understand concepts, since they are the ones doing the writing, organization, and solution.

Sometimes, the students will all write on the same topic. When we were studying the Arctic, they wanted to write problems about snowflakes. Carly wrote the following problem that Dave solved:

> Your snowflake has to have six sides. At the end of each side it has to have a circle. The sides have to be at least an inch apart.
>
> Now, get the colors: blue, red, and green.
>
> Color 1/3 of it green, 1/3 of it blue, and 1/3 of it red.
>
> What does your snowflake look like?

Figure 2.8 shows Alissa's problem solved by Kiersten.

The kids often write problems similar to the ones I write for them. Kyle wrote and solved the problem in Figure 2.9 during math workshop one morning.

Figure 2.8

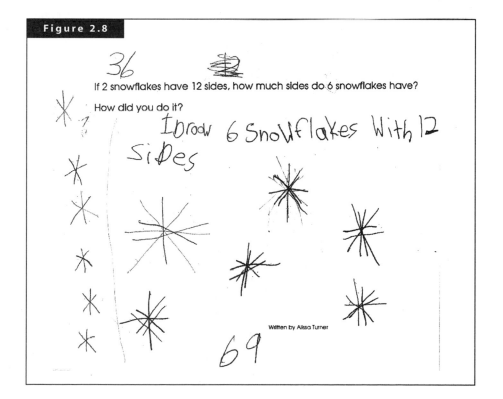

If 2 snowflakes have 12 sides, how much sides do 6 snowflakes have?

How did you do it?

I Drow 6 Snowflakes With 12 Sides

Written by Alissa Turner

Figure 2.9

Megan wrote the following problem when she was in third grade:

■ Art Time Math

There is a classroom with 60 bottles of paint, and 18 are 1/2 full. And 20 are 1/4 full, and 20 are 1/6 full, and the rest are full.

Then how many full bottles can you make?

We all worked on Megan's problem for a long time. It's hard! Then, when she was in fourth grade, she changed the problem to make it even more challenging:

■ Blue Paint Problem

In the art room there are 58 bottles of blue paint. Nine are 1/2 full, 12 are 1/4 full, 16 are 3/4 full, 18 are 1/3 full, and the rest are all the way full.

If you were to pour the paint into the least amount of bottles as possible, how many would there be?

Megan actually used this problem to share during her portfolio conference in fourth grade and had her mother solve it.

Sometimes, a child will come up with a problem that I think the whole class should solve. Jeff was working on understanding fractions during Calendar, and he came up to me one day during math workshop.

"Jill, I made this drawing and wrote different fractions about the people. See?"

"Cool, Jeff. Hey, can you draw them again on a different piece of paper? I'll copy it, and you can pass it out tomorrow during daily fractions at Calendar. Then you can look them over. How does that sound?"

"Yeah, I can do that!" And off Jeff went to redraw his people. Figure 2.10 shows Kyle's solution to Jeff's problem.

During our study of the 1940s one week of math workshop was devoted to writing problems that had to do with aspects of our study. The kids wrote problems, solved each other's problems, and during our exhibit night for the 1940s in the spring, we had all the problems out on a table for the parents to solve. The following are just a sampling of some of the problems the kids wrote during that time:

> If you had six family members in hiding in your house and two more came in, how many people would be hiding? Explain. [Mary]

> If you hide a family from January 8, 1942, to May 8, 1945, how long did you hide them? Explain. [Chris]

Figure 2.10

$\frac{4}{9}$ HAVe STRiPeD SHiRtS

$\frac{4}{9}$ HAVe HAtS ON

$\frac{1}{9}$ ARe liGHTNiNG BOlTS

$\frac{8}{9}$ HAVe ARMS BeHiND theRe BACK.

> You have 12 dishes, and you will need 1/4 of them in your secret room. So how many would you need in your secret room and how many in the kitchen? Explain. [Ashley]

> The power went out, and you do not have any electricity ration stamps left. The heat goes off, and it is very cold. One of the parents got sick; so did Kimberly and Kathryn. Megan had a bottle of medicine. The adult had to take 3 teaspoons and kids take 1 1/2 teaspoons. How much would they take in a week? Explain. [Kathryn]

Besides having kids write problems to solve, I try to encourage my students to pose problems that arise. For instance, when we are sharing and there is a confusing explanation, I urge my students to question what is being explained and shared, to pose new situations or a different way of looking at a problem, or to share an idea to expand on a problem. Just writing problems isn't enough. They often question my solutions and my ideas. I encourage this type of questioning from my students. I remember a project my younger students were working on that had a required area. Most of the kids were drawing the required area on graph paper using a rectangle. But Tessia challenged herself by asking about shape rather than area.

"Well, everyone is making rectangles to fit the area. I was wondering if I could take the area, and keep it the right number, but make it fit into the shape I want," Tessia asked.

"Can you explain that further? It sounds like a wonderful question, but I'm not sure I understand. Does anyone else?" I asked.

"Well, let's say I want my shape to be like this." She drew a shape on the whiteboard that looked like pyramid. "If I have the shape in my mind, I was wondering how I would get the area to fit my shape." There was her question; that was the problem she posed to herself. She did go and work this out. It took a few days, but she was persistent and came up with the area she needed for the shape she wanted.

Other Stuff

And then there are those pieces of work that fit into all or none of the categories I have mentioned, like the design books by my fourth, fifth, and sixth graders. This was an activity that my friend and colleague Alice Cotton had done with her fourth and fifth graders. I asked her if I could use it because it looked like so much fun to do. Each step of the problem had a mathematical part and an artistic part. I modified what she had done, and the following is what the kids were given to complete:

■ Design Book
Use any type of paper to complete your design book. Neatness counts.

1. Draw a shape that has an area of 18 square units but is not a rectangle or a square. How many sides does it have?
   This shape is part of a carpet design: 2/3 of the pattern is in shades of the same color. Color how it would look on the carpet.

2. Draw a polygon with four sides. Color each square unit inside it a different color. Use an equal number of warm and cool colors. What is the area of the shape in square units? What is the perimeter?

3. Draw a 4 × 9-unit rectangle. What is the area? Color 1/3 of the rectangle a blend of red and blue. What is 1/3 of the area? What color did you get?

4. Draw two 6 × 6-unit arrays.
   These are tiles. One tile needs to have a border that is only 1/4 of the size of one of the square units. The border should be in a decorative pattern. The other tile should be a complement of the first tile (the same but in a color that complements it).

5. Make a shape that has five sides with two sides that are parallel. Color the parallel lines thick purple, and color the rest of the shape yellow, including the inside.

6. Make a shape that has an area of 6 1/2 units. Now make a shape that is similar to this one. Turn them into a family with one parent and one child. Turn the shapes into illustrations of this family. Use shading and detail.

7. Draw a right triangle with an area of 8 square units. Describe how you knew it had an area of 8 square units. Are the other angles obtuse or acute? Turn this triangle into some sort of animal. [Figure 2.11 shows Dave's solution to this step.]

Figure 2.11

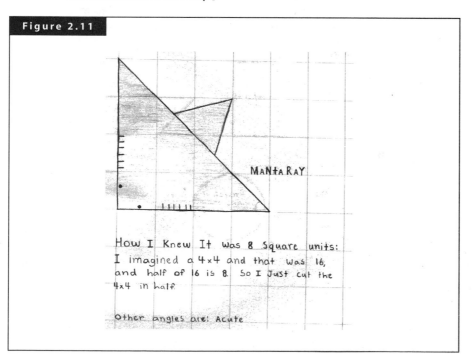

MANTA RAY

How I Knew It was 8 Square units:
I imagined a 4x4 and that was 16,
and half of 16 is 8. So I Just cut the
4x4 in half.

Other angles are: Acute

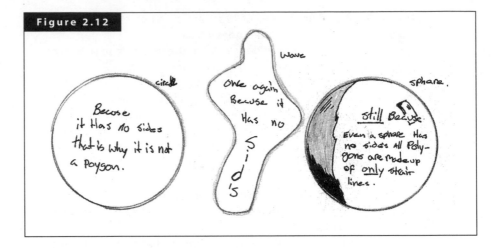

Figure 2.12

circle

Becose it Has no sides that is why it is not a Poygon.

Wave

Once again Becuse it Has no S i d 's

sphare.

still Becuse. Even a sphare Has no sides All Polygons are made up of only stair lines.

8. Make three shapes that are not polygons. In the middle of each shape, write why they aren't polygons. Then outline the shapes in different colors. [Figure 2.12 shows Sean's solution to this step.]

9. Make a shape that has one obtuse angle. Label this angle and then color the inside of the obtuse angle section the color of a rising sun. Label the other angles. Are they right angles or acute angles? Color the inside of the acute angles the color of the midday sun and the right angle, if there is one, the color of a setting sun.

10. Draw a circle that has a diameter of at least 5 inches. Draw at least five concentric circles inside the first one. Draw different patterns around the outside of each circle.

11. Create your own page for the design book. Write the design requirements and do it.

12. Make a table of contents for the book.

13. Make a cover for your design book that includes a title and the author. Make a cover design that fits your design book that is attractive and neat. Put pages 1–12 into the book, and bind it in some way or staple it. Make sure all pages are in order.

The older children also put together mini-math portfolios. (I called them portfolios because everything they did was put into a manila folder.) I wrote this just as a small problem, and the kids really did nice work on them. It was interesting for me to see who could do more than one solution for the same problem, and I learned a lot about how my students solve equations they write for themselves. I chose to focus on number and whole number computation for this particular math workshop project. We had been doing a lot of work on geometry at the time, and I wanted the kids to shift gears and focus on number equations. I was looking for more than accuracy on this project. I wanted to see how detailed their explanations would be.

Here are the instructions for the mini-portfolio:

For math workshop this week you are going to put together a mini-port-folio. It will need to have several items in it, and you can decide how you show them.

For example, let's say for multiplication I decide to show how I multiply 35 × 28. I can do it two different ways. I can make up an algorithm, and I can also do an array (showing 35 across and 28 down and counting up the arrays inside).

Here is the list of requirements you will need to show in your mini-portfolio:

■ Multiplication—at least a two-digit number by a two-digit number. [Figure 2.13 shows Dave's work on this item.]

Figure 2.13

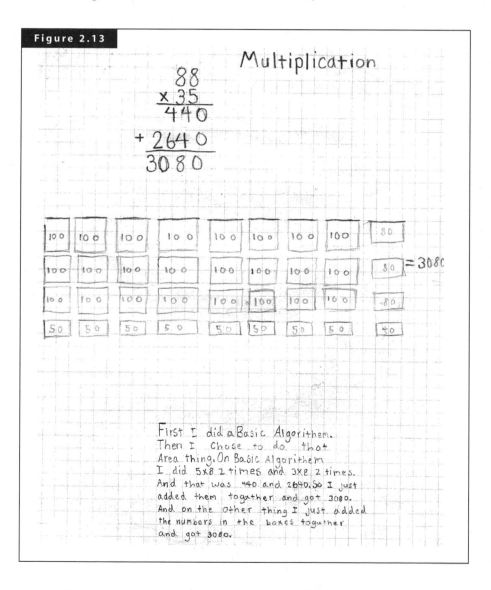

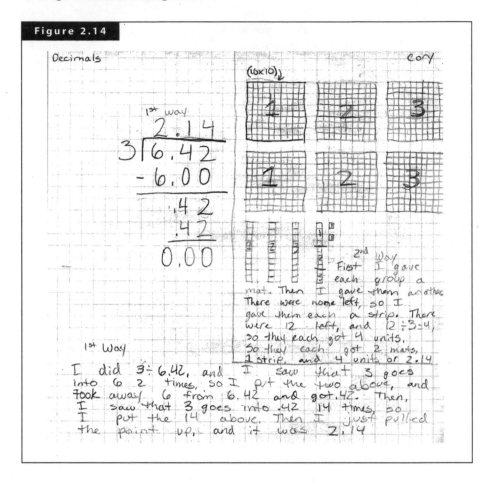

Figure 2.14

- Division—at least a two-digit number somewhere in the problem.
- Fraction—addition or subtraction of two fractions.
- Decimals—addition, subtraction, multiplication, or division. [Figure 2.14 shows Cory's work on this item.]
- Three written problems that you solve. The problems need to be about area and perimeter, money, and travel. [Figure 2.15 shows Kim's work on this item.]

This mini-portfolio needs to be very neat and well organized. Your problems need to have very detailed explanations with your solutions.

One year, my younger students worked on a number study for the entire year. They each chose a number at the beginning of the year, and they would periodically be asked to do specific things with their numbers. Some of the things they were asked to do were as follows:

- Draw all the arrays you can for your number.
- Do "ways to make" with your number.

Figure 2.15

Area and Perimiter

Jill wanted to plant a garden.
She has a small area to plant
it. But she needs to messure it
and find the area so she can
derside it up for different plants.
What is the P. and A. ?

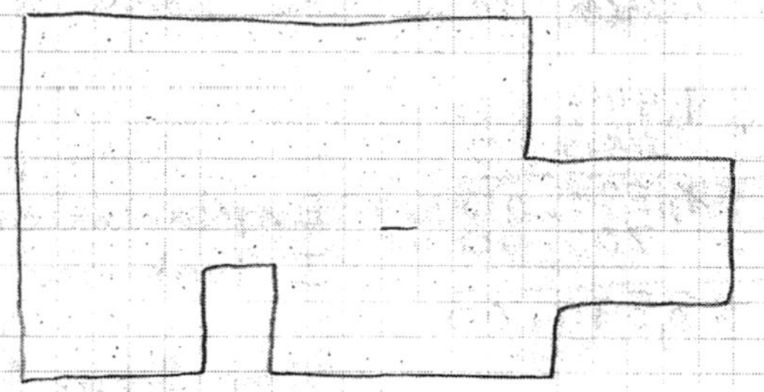

P = 11 × 5 × 3 × 2 × 3 × 8 × 2 × 5 × 4 × 6 × 4 × 14 sq.ft.

A = 160 sq. ft.

Explanation: I counted the little squares all
around the shape and pretended they were
sq. ft. Then For the A I counted all the squares
inside the shape.

Money

Rachel won the lottery. She one
$ 9,999. She gave 400.00 away to
Jamie and $700.00 away to Kim.
How much dose she have left?

$ 9,999.00
−   400.00
8 9,1599.00
−   700.00
$ 8,899.00

Explanation:
I took away 400.
and got 89,599.00
then from that took
away 700. and got
$ 8,899.00

- Draw your number on tens paper.
- What is your number tripled?
- What is your number quadrupled?
- What is your number halved?
- What is your number divided into sixths?
- Start at 35. How do you get to your number?
- Start at −15. How do you get to your number?

There were dozens of other things they worked on during the year with their numbers. It was interesting to observe how attached the kids became to their numbers. Often they would come to school and tell me that they had seen their numbers somewhere, like on a sign on the street. One child, whose number was 24, said that she discovered she had 24 spoons in her silverware drawer.

Just for the Fun of It

Sometimes, it's fun to just study something or learn about something that has absolutely nothing to do with curriculum guides or benchmarks. I remember when Aisha was studying non-Euclidean geometry in one of her graduate school classes. I was intrigued by this because, to tell you the truth, I had never even heard of non-Euclidean geometry. So I asked her to talk to me about it. I was totally into it and decided to have my kids experience some of the things I was learning from Aisha. Non-Euclidean geometry is all about looking at geometry on a different plane, for instance, the surface of a sphere. I began our talk with the class with the following question: "Who knows what a line is?"

"It's something that goes from here to there," Chris said.

"It's straight," said Mary.

"A line is like a pencil," Katie said.

"OK, so a line is straight, goes from here to there, and is like a pencil. Anything else? I want you to get a partner and write about lines. Write where you find lines, and what a line means. We'll get back together in about 15 minutes." Off went my first, second, and third graders to begin a study on non-Euclidean geometry. When we got back together, we discussed line again. I read them a few definitions of line from math textbooks. One book said that a line was a never-ending straight path. We talked about this definition, and the kids practiced drawing lines between two points and walking between two points. Many of the kids said that a line was the shortest distance between two points. They proved that the definition from the textbook was correct and that their definition was accurate, and they were comfortable with it. They also came up with their own definitions.

Then I gave each pair a toilet paper roll tube and a small piece of string. "OK, hold your tube up and with your pen draw a dot on one side of the tube close to the end of the tube," I said. "Now, turn the tube over so the dot is on the bottom, and draw another dot on the other side of the tube. So, you should have a dot on the right side of the top and on the left side of the bottom of the tube. Now, take your string and put it between the two points. What do you see?"

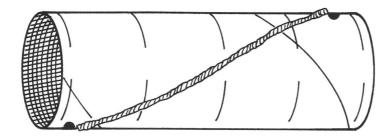

"It's a squiggly line," said Mary.

"It's not straight," said Kathryn.

"Oh, it's not straight? So, is this a line?" I asked. This set off a wonderful discussion. We talked about the textbook definition of line.

"Well, I think it is a line because the definition of a line is the shortest distance between two points, right? Well, the string is the shortest distance between these two points, so it must be a line. Is the textbook wrong?" Kyle asked.

"I think the textbook is right. But what does this tell you?" I asked.

We talked about lines on different planes, and I introduced the name Euclid and the term *non-Euclidean geometry*. We experimented with lines on spheres, cubes, and other 3-D shapes. We also experimented with triangles and circles on different planes.

Now, I realize that young kids don't need to know about non-Euclidean geometry. Heck, I made it into my mid-thirties without ever hearing the term. But it opened my eyes to new ideas. That's what learning is all about, and I was excited and wanted to share it with my students. It also opened their eyes, and when the standardized test came in the spring, and one question asked "Which of these is a line?" my kids could question the validity of the test! They knew that what a line is sometimes depends on the surface on which it is placed.

That same year we learned about the five Platonic solids. We built them, discussed where we could find them, watched a movie about them, and figured out their duals.

The kids work on a variety of problems all through the year. So when we are ready to work on our big project in the spring, I know that they have had as much experience with problem solving and as much exposure to all aspects of mathematical thinking as possible.

I don't think you need to abandon your curriculum and start writing problems tomorrow. It has taken me a long time to gain the confidence to do so and the knowledge of why I teach math the way I do. When I started, I began writing problems that revolved around what we were studying. Think about what you are studying with your students and try writing a problem that uses the information you are learning about. From there, you can add a multistep problem and some open-ended activities. Start out slowly. And, again, keep track of how your students respond and what you learn from them.

Active Practice

Learning should engage students both intellectually and physically. They must become active learners, challenged to apply their prior knowledge and experience in new and increasingly more difficult situations. Instructional approaches should engage students in the process of learning rather than transmit information for them to receive. Middle-grade students are especially responsive to hands-on activities in tactile, auditory, and visual instructional modes.

—NCTM Curriculum Standards

The term *workshop* has been used to define many learning situations over the last several years. This term was introduced to me through Nancie Atwell's written work about writing workshop. Yet, it has come to mean different things to different teachers and educators. My first official workshop was a writing workshop. Many teachers like myself used the ideas of Nancie Atwell and Don Graves as a springboard for creating a time where our students could experience the writing process.

Writing workshop is a time for my students to explore written language by practicing concepts they are learning. They choose topics to write about, experiment with different genres, share their drafts with other children, edit and revise their pieces, work on final copies, publish pieces, have conferences with me, and collaborate with their classmates. In our room, writing workshop is not a quiet time of day. The kids are talking about writing—their writing. There is movement as kids have conferences with each other and collaborate with one another. If you were to walk into our room during writing workshop, you would see children busy at work, not sitting quietly at desks.

The problem with certain words is that their meanings tend to change depending on who's saying them. It is confusing to be learning about new ideas and new terms and then to go into classrooms where those terms seem to mean something else than what you are learning about. Kathy, the parent of one of my students, worked as an aide at a middle school while getting her master's degree in teaching. She has had a child in my room for the past five years and associated the term *writing workshop* with what her children did in my room. So she was confused by what she saw in some of the language arts classes where she worked as an aide. "These classes say they are doing writing workshop, but it looks like they are just using the term to make it fit a teacher-directed situation. They are taking writing out of context, using the term *writing workshop* to teach a five-paragraph essay. Those kids are not being allowed to choose their own topics, to collaborate, or even to share their work. How is that a writing workshop?"

To make myself clear here, when I use the term *workshop*, I am referring to a time when my children make choices, collaborate, discuss, share, think, and rethink—at math time no less than at writing time.

I define any learning workshop as a time when children can explore, experience, practice, share, and discover new ideas. I have learned that the environment of the classroom goes hand in hand with the workshop. I assume that my classroom will be filled with busy workers who are free to move about the room. My learning workshops are not neat, quiet times; they are most often messy, and they are always filled with discussion and movement. Therefore, I set up my classroom in a way that will support this philosophy. My room is furnished with tables and couches bought at thrift stores (see my book *A Room with a Different View*). The children are encouraged to make choices about where they work. I do not assign work places for my students. Learning with whom and where to work is an important step in becoming an independent learner. I expect my children to know and understand what they are working on and why.

Many visitors to my room comment on the fact that they notice all the children working, doing what they are "supposed" to be doing. Even though it is noisy, they comment, the type of noise they hear sounds productive: kids discussing. They also comment that my children, when asked, always know why they are doing what they are doing. In her book *A Workshop of the Possible*, Ruth Hubbard writes, "When I visit a classroom for the first time, I often ask children to explain to me what's going on, or 'what usually happens now.' If kids can't tell me, it usually means they are dependent on the teacher to orchestrate all the movement in the class. They aren't able to be independent and therefore flexible in their use of time."

In my classroom, a workshop is not the time for the kids to sit quietly at desks or a time when skills are practiced in isolation. It is the time when my kids practice and use what they are learning, to learn more. I believe that learning should be active and challenging. The workshop approach is what I have found best matches my beliefs about learning.

The introduction to our math workshop is Calendar. We do an extensive calendar each morning for 20 to 35 minutes. Chapters 3 and 4 describe our calendar time and our math workshop.

3

Calendar

When I began teaching 16 years ago, I set up my calendar time by what I had learned in undergraduate school. Everyone did Calendar, and that's why I decided to, but I did not understand the full importance of it. *Math Their Way* (Baretta-Lorton 1995) was the first book I read that influenced my early calendar activities. This was a very influential book in my early teaching years, but still I had no understanding of the amount of mathematical thinking that could go into Calendar. I thought the purpose of Calendar was to learn the days of the week or to know how many days are in each month. These are important things to learn but minor compared to what can be done in Calendar.

I remember the year I took Calendar down. I threw it away and stopped doing it for the rest of the school year. We needed the wall space, and our Calendar seemed to take up valuable room. I recall a churning in my stomach, a sort of guilt for what I had done. I couldn't explain it at the time, it seemed so odd to me, but now I realize why I was feeling that way. I began to rethink the way Calendar was organized and presented to my kids. By observing the kids during this time, I not only came to understand the importance of Calendar every day but also what children are capable of doing during that block of morning time. So many elementary and early childhood teachers incorporate a calendar time into their days. It's an old classic.

Over the years, I have read many books and math curricula that talk about calendar time, but it wasn't until I put the books away and just began to closely observe my children that I learned the most. It was then that I began to look at Calendar as much more than just getting together as a class to name the days of the week, count how many days we've been in school, or pattern the days of the week on a large blank calendar. It was when I stepped back and observed how they were able to challenge themselves with complex ideas, learn from each other, and take the responsibility of organizing it all, that I truly began to understand how crucial this activity is.

Each day there is a child who leads Calendar. Kids sign up for a day they want to lead. The leader is responsible for calling us over, passing out the calendar books, making sure everyone is paying attention, calling on kids to do certain activities, and asking questions. There is one leader each day. I sit back and participate with the rest of the class. It is very exciting when a child new to the class leads Calendar for the first time. The kids usually help him through it. I remember the first time Cody led Calendar as a first grader. When he had finished, all the kids clapped!

Since I know I will want the kids to make and set up the calendar, I often ask a few older kids to take parts of the display to make over the summer. For example, I asked Josh one August to make the blank calendar out of posterboard. I then laminated it and have used that one for several years. Usually, during the first day of school, I will have other kids make signs that go with all the activities as well. There are a few unchanging activities that we do daily throughout the year, and there are some activities that change.

Unchanging Activities

The following activities are those we do every day consistently without much change.

The Calendar

The actual calendar is a blank monthly calendar made out of posterboard with the days of the week written across the top of the boxes that will eventually hold the dates of the month. During Calendar, the leader usually asks, "What day is it today?" and calls on a child who has raised her hand. The leader then writes the number on the calendar. She then asks the audience questions like How many more days until the end of the month? How many days ago did we have a weekend? Is this number odd or even? What is this number doubled? The questions change daily depending on who is leading.

If there is a pattern on the calendar for that month, the leader will fill in the pattern or ask someone in the audience to guess what the pattern is. The patterns are usually drawn right onto the calendar. The patterns are thought up by a child who has requested to do a pattern for that month. At the beginning of the month, before the pattern has been established, the child who invented it writes the sequence every day until the pattern has been discovered by the class. After that, the leader asks, "Who can tell me what to put up for the pattern?"

How Many Days?

This activity has been refined over the years. It is one of the best ways my students learn and internalize the concept of place value. On the bulletin board next to the calendar there are six containers. (I have used french fry containers, small yogurt tubs, and take-out food containers.) They are arranged in two rows, three in each row. Each box is labeled, from the right: *ones, tens, hundreds.* Under each container is a small pad of Post-it notes. Next to the small Post-it pad of the container labeled *ones* is a large Post-it pad. Next to each row of containers is a sign that has been written by a child: *How many days in school?* and *How many days do we have left in school?* At the beginning of the year, I find out how many days there are in the school year and put that many popsicle sticks or straws into the tubs marked *days left in school?* The sticks are bundled into groups of ten with a rubber band. The hundreds bundle contains ten bundled groups of ten, not a loose group of 100 sticks. (I either put them in already bundled in the right way or on the first day have a group of kids do the bundling.) As the leader gets to this phase of Calendar, he asks one member of the audience to come up and move a stick from one container to the other. For instance, if there are 125 days left in school, the "days left in school" containers look like this:

And, if we have been in school 97 days the "days in school" container look like this:

The person chosen by the leader will move a stick from the ones container of "days left in school" and put it into the ones container of "days in school." After all sticks have been moved, the leader pulls off the Post-it notes that need to be changed to match the new number of sticks in each container. After that, the leader questions the audience again. At the beginning of the year the questions are usually pretty general, such as What number will tomorrow be? but after some time has passed and through listening to each other, the kids' questions grow more complex. Some questions have been What does the 9 mean in 97? What does the 1 mean in 125? How many more days until we are at 107 days? Are the numbers odd or even? These questions, especially those asked about the meaning of the numbers, are important for learning about place value and number.

Observing the movement of the sticks helps the kids to see the trading process of place value. If there are no more sticks in the ones box, they learn that they must take a bundle from the tens container, take the rubber band off, and borrow a stick from that bundle. I have observed kids actually referring back to this activity of Calendar when they are working on a problem during math workshop. I remember hearing Jessica tell a friend, "It's just like taking the rubber bands off at Calendar. You need more ones, so pretend you're taking the rubber band off and then give yourself one of those and put the rest back. That would be nine left over from the ten." Her explanation helped her partner make the connection to what she was trying to do as she solved a problem involving subtraction.

Ways to Make

A small whiteboard is used for the "ways to make" section of Calendar. When it is time to do "ways to make," the leader writes the number to be used on the whiteboard. The number usually corresponds to the day of the month. If it is the eighth day of the month, for instance, the leader will write 8 on the whiteboard. She then calls on the audience for ways to make the number 8.

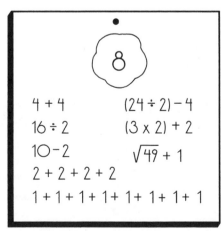

The individual levels of the students become apparent during "ways to make." It is a time when the kids can fully challenge themselves. Second grader Ross was called on during "ways to make" on the seventh day of the month. He said, "The square root of 49."

"Wow. How did you know that Ross?" I asked.

"My dad and I were doing square root last night."

"How do you do it? Can you explain square root to us?" I asked.

"Yeah, sure. It's just double the number kind of. Like, 7×7 is 49, so the square root of 49 is 7. But it's not plus, only times." And from then on, the kids began doing square root in very creative ways. Kyle's equation for the number 8 was (square root of 49) + 1. For the number 4, he wrote (square root of 1) + 3. Paige's equation for the number 9 was (square root of 100) take away 2 plus 1. It became a game after a while. The kids would try to figure out what the square root equation would be for each number. Some would get a calculator, and others would do the multiplication in their heads. Shanti figured out that the square root of 196 was 14 by multiplying 14×14 on a calculator, and she told the others this on the fourteenth day of the month during "ways to make."

Paige became very interested in negative numbers and would often share equations she had come up with that dealt with negative numbers. From her interest, we discussed negative numbers, and more kids began to construct equations with negative numbers.

Today's Array

This was an idea I originally got from Aisha, who learned it from *Opening Eyes to Mathematics* (Arcidiacono, Head, and Pollett 1995). Knowing what an array is and being able to visualize an array is crucial in the early elementary grades. The whole concept of multiplication and division is so much easier to understand and visualize if kids have a solid understanding of what an array is.

An array is any square or rectangle where the dimensions of the sides are defined. For example, the following is an array for the number 8:

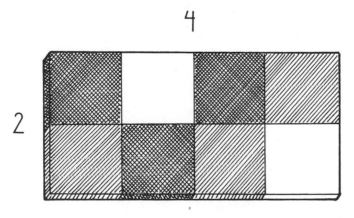

On the bulletin board there is a cookie sheet. In a container nearby, there are tiles or squares with magnetic tape attached to one side. During the "today's array" phase of Calendar, the leader calls on a child to do the array for the day. The number corresponds to the date. The child moves that number of tiles around on the cookie sheet until he has found all the arrays for the number that he can. Here are the arrays for number 8:

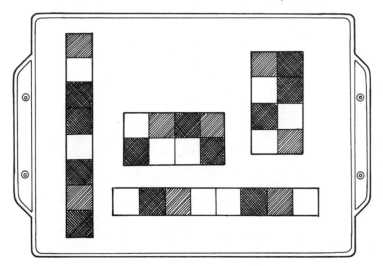

The leader then asks the child to write the dimensions of each array down on a piece of paper. They verbalize these dimensions by using the word *by*. For an array that has dimensions of 4 and 2, the leader says, "4 by 2" but writes 4×2. The kids, especially the third-grade students, discover the connection to the multiplication and division symbols over time.

Sometimes the number has several arrays, and the person chosen to do the array is slower coming up with a solution than the pace of Calendar allows. The leader will let that child complete the job while Calendar continues. So we sometimes have a child working on an array while we are doing another part of Calendar. When the child has finished, we simply return to it. If the child has missed some of the arrays, the leader asks the audience if they can see what is missing. If the leader doesn't catch the missing arrays, it is up to the audience to catch them. If no one does, I might step in and ask questions.

Using arrays during Calendar helps the kids get used to a visual model of multiplication and division.

Area and Perimeter

Doing area and perimeter every day allows the kids to become familiar with a concept they will use forever. It also helps for some of the large building problems we undertake during the school year (see Chapter 5). I put up a new piece of 1 inch × 1 inch graph paper each morning. At the beginning of the year, I draw the picture to be used, but after a few months I let the leader of Calendar for that day draw the shape to be used.

I begin the year with simple drawings that will be easy to count and easy to see:

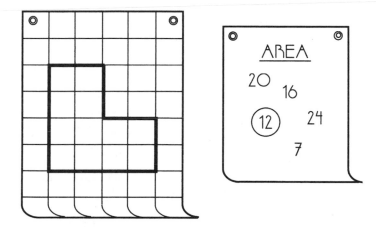

The leader asks the audience, "What's the area?" and calls on those who have their hands up. The leader writes down *all* the responses until all who want to share have done so. She then counts up the squares inside the shape. The rest of the class usually chimes in and helps . . . and circles the correct written number or writes the answer next to the responses.

The leader does the same procedure for perimeter, except when the children count they usually write each dimension first and then add up each side:

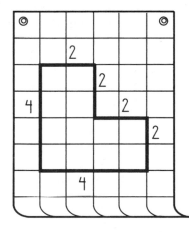
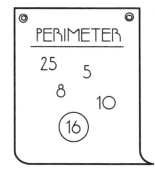

Daily Fraction

I am putting "daily fraction" here as an unchanging activity because we do some sort of fraction every day. Fractions seem to be left out of many elementary classrooms, and it is a concept that kids can understand.

Every month we change the type of fraction activity, but we never leave out a fraction activity. The leader writes what a student says on a piece of paper placed under the sign labeled *Daily Fraction*. If the leader for that day is a more experienced writer, we might have seven or eight fractions written. If the leader is an inexperienced writer, we might have two or three written. At first, the kids write exactly what was shared. For instance, if the fraction being shared is 2/7, the person sharing will usually say, "2 out of 7" and the leader will actually write the words *out of*.

I have found that my young students understand fractions first by using the words *out of*. Later on, we will begin writing fractions numerically. By seeing the written fraction with the numerator and the denominator, and by verbalizing the fraction using the term *out of*, the kids begin to see the relation between the two. Later on in the year, I might ask, "What's another way to say 4 out of 5?" I look for the language "four-fifths." From there, I will ask that both ways be verbalized.

Here are some of the fraction activities we have done in the past. Each month we do a different one for the entire month.

People Fractions. The kids come up with fractions that have to do with the people in our class. For example, they might say, "3 out of 28 people have on hats." The leader might write 3/28 have on hats.

Picture Fractions. I put up a picture from a magazine, and the kids create fractions about the picture. Let's say it is a picture of three children, one of whom is feeding a dog. A child might say, "One out of three kids is feeding a dog."

Map Fractions. I put up a map of some sort. When we were studying the 1940s, I displayed a map of Europe. The kids came up with fractions about the map. For example, some responses were "5/36 countries are touching Germany," and "about 1/3 of Russia is in Europe."

Name Fractions. Each day of the month we wrote a name of a child in the class and did fractions with that name. For example, for Chelsea, a response might have been, "Two out of seven letters are e's."

Pattern Block Fractions. This idea first came to me from Aisha when she was doing a math workshop session with my younger students. I decided to bring some of what I had learned from her to Calendar. The possibilities with pattern blocks are endless. The following are four pattern blocks.

green   blue   red   yellow
triangle   diamond   trapezoid   hexagon

To introduce the idea of pattern blocks at daily fractions, I put up one pattern block, and the kids share what fractions they can about that block. For instance, one day I might put up a blue diamond. The kids think up fractions for the blue diamond during the "daily fraction" part of Calendar. Possible responses might be, "It is 1/3 of a yellow hexagon" and "1/2 of it is a green triangle."

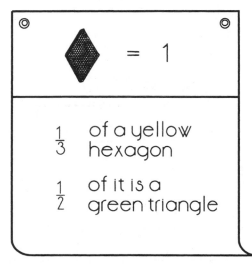

After we have gone through each pattern block in that way, I begin to make the problems more challenging. For example, I may put up two green triangles and write that together they now have a value of 1. The kids then work out what the values of the other pattern blocks would be. Possible responses for that problem might be, "A blue diamond equals 1" and "Three green triangles equal 1 1/2."

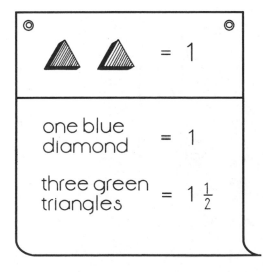

Still more challenging (and I wouldn't do this particular problem until the kids have had much experience with pattern block fractions) is putting up several different pattern blocks at once and giving that design a value. I might put up a yellow hexagon and a green triangle and give that design a value of 1. Possible responses to this might be, "One green triangle equals 1/7" and "Two red trapezoids equal 6/7."

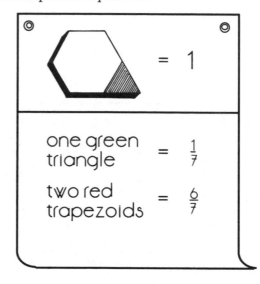

Egg Carton Fractions. I often use egg cartons as a manipulative to teach fractions. These work well at Calendar. An egg carton is put up on the bulletin board, and we do egg carton fractions. I use puff balls or colored squares to fill in the compartments of the egg carton. For instance, I might fill the egg carton with three yellow puff balls and the rest with red ones. Possible responses might be, "3/12 are yellow," "1/4 are yellow," and "3/4 are red."

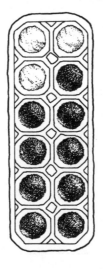
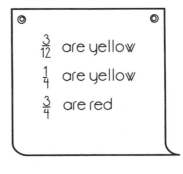

A variation of this is putting up two or three egg cartons at a time. I fill up all the compartments, and the kids create fractions in the same way.

Fraction Strip Fractions. I also make little fraction strips to use at Calendar and at math workshop. These are paper strips that have different parts of the strip shaded in:

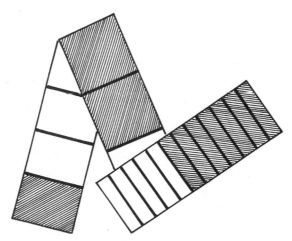

I have used these at Calendar in a variety of ways. I might put up one strip, and the kids create fractions for that one piece. The following example is from Kyle's calendar book as he wrote solutions for the fraction strip that had four out of six blocks shaded: 4/6 are shaded, 2/6 are not shaded, 1/6 has a pin in it (the pin used to attach the bar to the bulletin board), 1/6 is the top, 1/6 is the bottom.

I have also used two fraction strips at a time, and the kids come up with equivalent fractions. Some responses to the following strips were, "2/5 = 4/10" and "3/5 = 6/10."

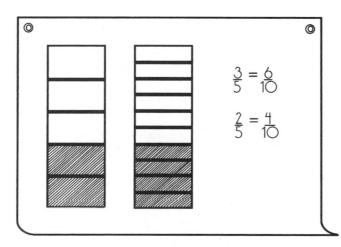

Every month, we do a different variety of daily fraction. This daily exposure to fractions has been significant in improving my students' ability to solve more complex problems during math workshop.

Varying Activities

Many activities are added throughout the school year. Some of these will remain part of Calendar for the rest of the year, and others just for a month or two.

Base 5 and Base 10 Pieces

Base 5 and base 10 pieces are added underneath the "days in school" containers. With blue tack or tape, a piece is added each day. Having both base systems next to each other gives the kids a chance to compare the two and see how they are related.

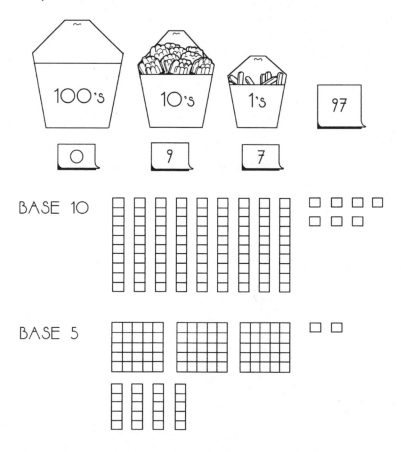

Money

Since working with money is such a great way to help children with place value and grouping numbers, I use money at Calendar as well. To the "days in school" section, we might add money. If we have been in school for 97 days, for example, the kids would move coins around in pockets or baggies attached to the bulletin board and write 97 cents. The leader writes on a blank piece of paper a chart that shows the different coins. The audience gives examples for different combinations to make that amount of money, and the leader fills in the chart.

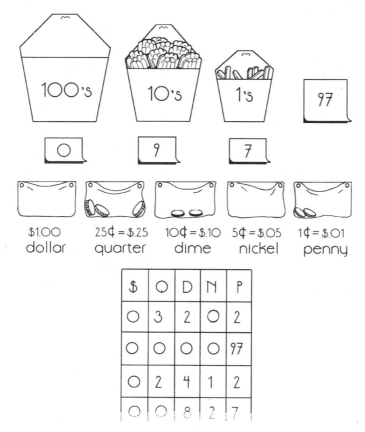

$	Q	D	N	P
O	3	2	O	2
O	O	O	O	97
O	2	4	1	2
O	O	8	2	7

Some kids also challenge themselves with this part of Calendar by making statements like, "Two dollars take away $1.03."

Time

On a small whiteboard I drew a clock using permanent marker. With an erasable pen, the leader will draw the hands and have a child say what time it is and write it on the board, or the leader might write the time and have the child draw the hands.

Calendar Books

The year I took down Calendar, I did so because I had noticed that not all the kids in class were attentive. Some of the less experienced mathematicians were lost, and the more experienced ones looked bored. So the following year I came up with the idea for calendar books.

Each child was given a blank book at the beginning of every month. Attached to the front was a blank calendar page. The book contained enough paper for one page per day for one month. These books are for the kids' use; I don't use them for assessment purposes and rarely look at them. At the beginning of Calendar, the leader passes out the calendar books. (I also have a calendar book and write in mine as the children do in theirs.)

I have discovered several benefits to these calendar books. First, they are a place for each child to process Calendar at his own pace. The more experienced mathematicians might write 15 to 20 "ways to make," while the less experienced ones may write two or three. They play with number and discover patterns. In their calendar books, the kids are free to practice these discoveries at their own pace and at their own level. Seven-year-old Jake wrote the following sequence for the number 7: $8 - 1$, $9 - 2$, $10 - 3$, $11 - 4$, $12 - 5$ . . . all the way up to $18 - 11$. Eight-year-old Shanti discovered the pattern for 11 and wrote in her book the following sequence: $22 \div 2$, $33 \div 3$, $44 \div 4$ and so on. Nine-year-old Kyle discovered a pattern with the number 7. He wrote during the seventh day of a month $14 \div 2$, $21 \div 3$, $28 \div 4$, . . . all the way up to $238 \div 34$. Also, the more experienced children might be able to write down all the activities we do during one Calendar day, while the less experienced can only write a few equations at "ways to make." Figures 3.1, 3.2, and 3.3 show two calendar pages and a cover.

Second, these books help with the attentiveness of the group as a whole. If the children aren't sharing, observing, or participating, they are writing. I have found that the books really help to create a quiet and concentrated time of the day.

The books are for the kids to write what they are experiencing at Calendar. Some children copy down what is being written by the leader, while others might write more or less than that. Some kids use the books to doodle in as they listen to others. This is important for some kids to do. I often doodle while I am listening to a speech or listening at a book reading. When kids doodle, it doesn't always mean they aren't paying attention.

The 30 minutes every morning devoted to Calendar has become an established part of our school day and an important, essential component of my math program. Letting the kids be in charge of setting up and leading it has only made this time stronger.

Even with the activities we do every day, each day is a different experience. Every leader has his own unique twist on how he leads the session and what questions he asks. The solutions and answers are always changing. I am not worried anymore about Calendar becoming a rote or stale part of

Figure 3.1

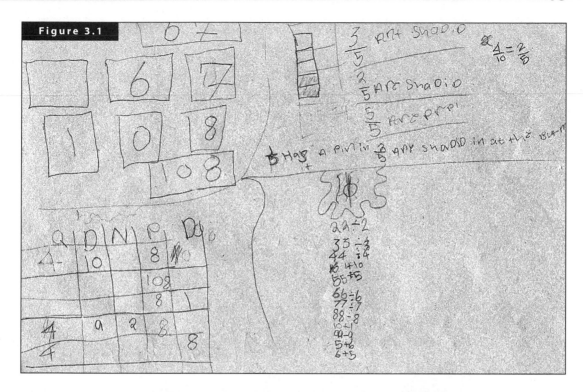

Figure 3.2

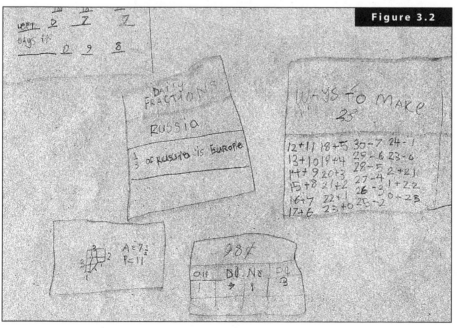

Figure 3.3

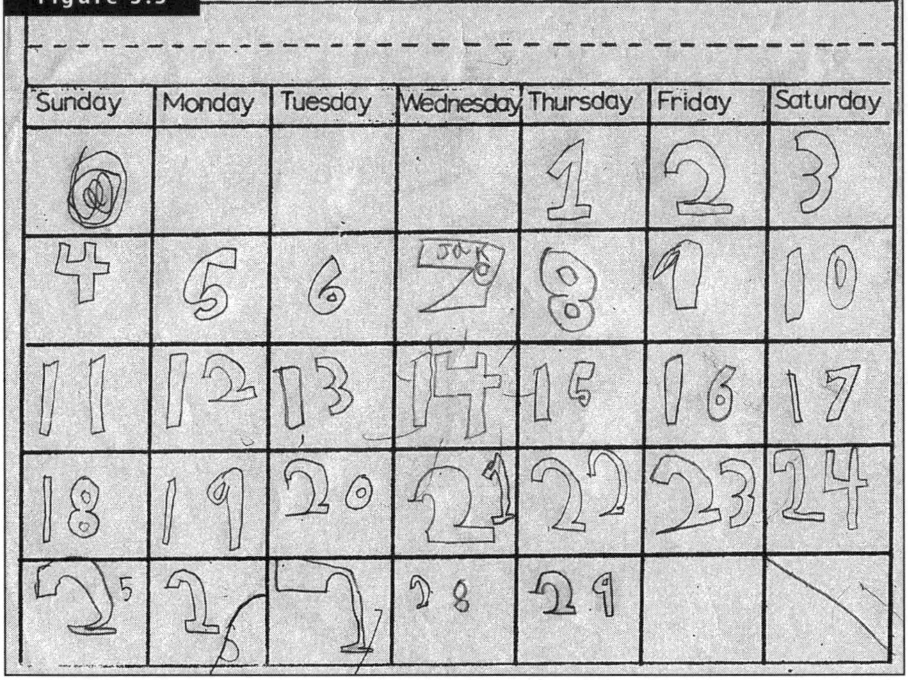

our day. Since some activities change every month, and I am always adding new ideas to Calendar, it stays fresh and new. It has become a part of the day that I do not dread anymore but look forward to.

I did not begin with calendar time that looked this complex. I don't think you need to go out tomorrow and change your calendar time to add every aspect I have described. I encourage teachers to gradually add something new, an aspect they found interesting and want to try. Starting a daily fraction might be a good place to begin. See how your students react, take notes on how it goes, and assess if this exposure to fractions on a daily basis helps your students learn the concept of fractions. I usually add more calendar activities in this manner. I ask if it is working for our class, if I find it helpful to my students, and what I am learning by doing it. Sometimes we stop certain activities because they didn't seem to work the way I had envisioned. It's important to question and evaluate the things you add to your own calendar time.

Calendar segues into math workshop. After the calendar books have been collected by the leader, the kids begin their math workshop for the day.

4

Math Workshop

Math workshop is very similar to writing workshop in that the children practice, collaborate, experiment, share, think, rethink, and have conferences with me. Similarly, the children are not working on one isolated skill or concept; they are working on many skills and concepts throughout the workshop. Some of the key issues in my learning workshops are choice, time, conferencing, sharing, and mini-lessons. Within those areas there are many similarities between a writing workshop and a math workshop, yet there are also differences. Below I have written fairly generally how these key issues are the same and how they differ. Throughout this chapter you will read about these key issues and how they weave through math workshop.

The Essentials

Choice

During writing workshop the children choose what to write about. My students are free to choose topics and genres, and to make decisions about when or when not to complete a piece of writing. That same choice is present in math workshop insofar as the children choose what strategies to use to help their thinking processes. The difference is that math workshop usually begins with a specific problem for the kids to solve. Their choice given that parameter is how to solve the problem. When they have completed their problem for that day, they may choose how they will spend the rest of the workshop time. If they don't finish the problem, they can work on it later that day or the following day.

During writing workshop the kids choose whom to work with. My students do not have assigned seats. They are free to collaborate with anyone they choose. This is not always the case, though, during math workshop. There are certain instances where I want to observe strategies certain children might use together. I often create groups or partnerships for the kids to work in. Depending upon the problem and what I want to learn from my students, I decide whether the kids will be able to choose whom they work with or be given a group or partnership. I used to worry about not always giving my students the freedom to choose who they work with. Yet I have come to believe that if I give my students enough chances to choose their own work groups and partnerships, they will respect my decision to take the choice away every now and then. When I assign them to work with someone, they get opportunities to work and learn with children whom they might not have chosen for themselves.

Time

It is essential to give an ample amount of time for any learning workshop. Writing workshop in our room usually lasts an hour to an hour and a half. The kids need time to explore, think, draft, write, share, collaborate, edit, revise, conference, and illustrate. Math workshop also lasts an hour to an hour and a half. In writing workshop the kids usually don't complete a piece of writing in one day; they can pick up where they left off during each workshop. In math workshop there is usually the expectation that they will complete the problem in one workshop. Of course, if we are working on a long project, the working time is extended. But generally the big problem for the day is completed during that day's math workshop.

Conferencing

During writing workshop the kids have formal and informal conferences with me and with each other. Formal conferences would include a publishing conference with me or a more involved editing conference. Informal conferences would include me simply asking the children to read me what they are working on and where they are going with their piece. The children also continually confer with their peers. There is a lot of discussion and movement during writing workshop.

During math workshop the kids also conference with me. I usually make sure to tell the children where I will be if they need guidance with a problem. This strategy works better for me than walking around the room and checking in with each child. Some children don't need me to check in with them every time we work on a problem, whereas others need me near them all the time as they build their confidence. Some kids just want to sit by me and know I'm there but never need to ask for help. Sometimes, my physical presence is all that's required.

Sharing

Every day after the actual writing, we have a whole-group sharing time to close writing workshop. Sharing is an essential part of the workshop. The kids get a chance not only to share their own work but to ask questions and give comments to others. This is true for math workshop as well: every math workshop ends with a whole-group sharing time. This is not simply for show and tell; it is a time to discuss strategies and ideas. In both the writing and the math workshops, each child does not get a chance to share every day. But in math workshop we can pull everyone into the discussion by figuring out how many kids used the same strategy or ideas to find a solution. Again, I stress the importance of this sharing time for learning by listening to others share their work and thinking.

Mini-Lessons

Our writing workshop does not always begin with a mini-lesson. I try to base mini-lessons on what comes up during the workshop. For instance, if I see a child experimenting with quotation marks, I may have a whole-group mini-lesson on quotation marks or just have a mini-lesson with a small group of children who could use more information on that skill. I usually save whole-group mini-lessons for the parts of writing, for instance, leads or character development.

During math workshop the mini-lessons often occur during sharing time. If someone has come up with a particularly interesting or helpful strategy, we often take time to explore it more closely. Usually, when the problem is handed out at the beginning of math workshop, we go over the choices the kids have for solving the problem. But I want my children to think about problems first, to explore possibilities, and to ask questions among themselves.

I hope that helps to clarify my thinking on the similarities and differences between my math and writing workshops. If it seems as though the workshops are complicated and messy, they are!

My writing workshop did not start out being the way I had imagined. It has taken me years to build on the ideas that were important to me. Take small steps at first. Maybe incorporate choice into your writing time. Observe how the kids react, how you respond to the changes, and what positive and negative aspects you notice. Then, refine the workshop, change it, expand it; experiment and take risks. A graduate student of mine recently told me about the first writing workshop she had tried with her first-grade class: "They loved it! At first I was so nervous to let them go on their own. I am used to giving them topics to write about. When I told them that they could write whatever they wanted, they wouldn't stop. At the end of the first day, they all asked me when we could do it again." Through the next few weeks, this teacher gradually felt more comfortable adding more to her workshop.

I've experimented with many different ideas during my workshops and have changed aspects of them every year; I suspect I always will. There are no easy rules to follow. What I have learned, though, is that my children have accomplished a great amount of learning in a workshop environment.

The Framework

I make sure I give a wide variety of problems to my students during math workshop. I remember that when I began teaching I would go through the concepts as they appeared in the textbook. I'd spend a few weeks on division and then go on to fractions, and so on. This practice of spending a few weeks on one specific concept seems to be very common. Yet, concentrating intensely on one concept isn't as meaningful or as essential for learning as incorporating the concepts children need to learn all the time, throughout the year. One year early in my teaching career we spent weeks on long division. This is such a hard and confusing algorithm for children to learn. Then, when the chapter ended and the kids seemed able to solve all of the 35 problems on a page, we went on to something else. Yet, months later, they couldn't even remember how to divide.

In order for kids to internalize concepts they need to practice using concepts recurrently. In other words, now I don't focus on multiplication for a month and then go on to division. I focus on all concepts all through the year. One day I might write a problem that involves division and fractions, and the next day I might write a problem that focuses on area and perimeter. Following are two examples of problems written during our 1940s study. These were given during math workshop the same week.

■ Factory Problem

There was a factory in Kidsville in 1942. Before the war, the factory was fully staffed: 64 men worked in it.

After the war began, only 1/4 of the men were left to work. How many men were then working in the factory?

But wait … the women of Kidsville said, "We can do it!" and they filled up the factory staff. How many women were needed to fully staff the factory?

Explain your solution.

■ Victory Garden: 2

Using the Victory Garden you drew, figure out the area and perimeter of the garden.

Imagine that you could double the size of your garden. What would the area and perimeter be then?

Explain your solution.

I give the kids as many concepts to work on as I can, as many times as possible. Children need to be able to move with ease between concepts they are learning. Not only does this keep all concepts fresh in their minds with less chance for them to forget what they have learned, but it seems much more realistic. Adults use a variety of mathematical concepts during a day; we don't add one day and divide another. We use fractions to figure out how to double a recipe, measurement to put in the ingredients, division to divide what was made, and multiplication to figure out how much we need. Mathematics is a collaboration of concepts.

It may sound as if it would be impossible for me to keep track of all the concepts to be covered, since I don't go in a prescribed sequence. I have a list of my district's requirements and the NCTM Standards, which I look over during the year. Some years we have focused on certain things more than other years. For instance, one year we focused on fractions longer than we did the next year because my students needed more work with fractions. I wish I could show you the form I use to keep track of it all, but I don't have one. I have a good memory and keep what I know in my head. I encourage you to make one, though, if organizational forms are useful to you. Perhaps keeping a list of the requirements and standards and checking off an item each time your kids have experience with it would be useful. A quick glance would then let you know if some areas have more checks than others.

So, when *do* I focus on a specific concept? I usually do so in the context of questions. For example, one problem I gave my first, second, and third graders dealt with equivalent fractions. Instead of saying, "OK, today we're going to work on equivalent fractions," I passed out the problem and let the questions evolve. From those questions we had mini-lessons on how to work with fractions with different denominators.

I'm not saying that it isn't good teaching practice to spend time on specific concepts; it is essential to do that. But I do think that teaching concepts in a strict order and a set time frame is detrimental. Frequent mini-lessons on a particular concept seem more appropriate than one large unit on the same concept.

The Tools

Besides the variety of concepts to be learned, there should also be a variety and choice of strategies for solving problems. Math manipulatives are as important to have in a classroom as books and paper are.

In my room the children have access to an ample number of manipulatives. They know that they may choose any manipulative to help them solve any problem. They can solve problems using manipulatives, pictures, drawings, or just their heads, provided they are able to write about how they solved the problems.

I have collected manipulatives for years. Some have been useful, and others haven't The manipulatives that I find the children use most often are

unifix cubes
pattern blocks
tens strips
geoboards
dice
calculators
compasses
egg cartons
colored square tiles
graph paper (all sizes)
rulers
colored pencils

My children use many specialized manipulatives as well, such as base 5 pieces, but the listed one are the ones I make sure to have plenty of. And these are for the children to use when they need to, they are not locked up in a cabinet. If there is a manipulative that we want and I don't have, we usually make it. A parent a few years back made me a class set of geoboards. I always make fraction pieces with the kids, and we keep plain wooden cubes handy for making dice.

The Workshop

It's hard to describe math workshop in a nice neat way because it is everchanging. I can tell you that math workshop lasts from 45 minutes to an hour and a half, comes after Calendar, and involves some sort of problem for the day. That is really all that is constant. My philosophy and the district guidelines are kept intact. But the actual structure of math workshop can take many different shapes depending on what we are working on. What we do, what we learn, whom we work with, where we work, and how we share are ever-changing.

Math workshop usually begins with a problem I have written for the kids to solve. They work on the problem independently, as partners, or in small groups. After the children have solved the problem, instead of coming to me and saying, "Jill, I'm done, now what?" they know what is expected of them. They use the time to explore and play with what they are learning. They choose games to play that I have taught them or they have created or learned somewhere else, they practice skills they are learning alone or with partners, they write problems to solve, they extend the problem they have just solved to be more challenging, and so on. They are surrounded by all the concepts and materials of math.

Mathematical Creativity

The games the children have created over the years range from board games to simple dice games. One nice thing about teaching a multiage class is that these games are passed down and reshaped over the years by the kids in the class. The older kids teach the younger kids a game or an activity, and the younger ones in turn modify the game in some way or other. As the child moves up grades in the class, he teaches that game to new kids, who in turn modify it. There are many games that have changed form over the years by this passing down "from generation to generation."

One such game is a trading game I taught the kids using colored tiles. Each tile is worth a different amount, and the object of the game is to get to 100. Let's say a green tile is worth 5 and a yellow tile is worth 10. If you had two greens, you could trade them in for a yellow. During math workshop over the years, the kids have created more challenging variations of the numbers and rules of that game.

"Jill, I made up a really cool game with the colored squares. Each color is a different amount. Like, red could be 5, blue could be 7, green could be 10, yellow could be 15. Then you spin the dice and take the colors that you need for the number on the dice," eight-year-old Ben told me one day.

"That's cool. But what if you spin and get an 8, then what would you do?" I ask. I could tell he didn't have a clue, but I waited for him to think about that question.

"Oh. Well, you would take a blue, and write 7 down on a piece of paper, and you could use the rest of it, the 1, on your next spin," he said.

"Good idea! Why don't you go play it that way, and see if it works."

I remember a fraction game a child made where the red pieces were worth 1/2, the blue were worth 1/4, the yellow were worth 2/4, and the green were worth 1. The child who created the game made a die by taking a wooden cube and writing 1/2, 1/4, 2/4, and 1 on the sides. The object of the game was to get to 5.

This is what math workshop is all about: kids being independent enough to challenge themselves and to accept challenges from me. There are dozens of games my kids have created with those little colored squares.

Nine-year-old Laura used the tiles to make a pattern problem. She had taken the idea from a problem I had posed to them and modified it for her problem. She placed the tiles in a pattern—blue, red, yellow, blue, red, yellow. She then numbered each tile in order and wrote questions to go with the pattern.

blue	red	yellow	blue	red	yellow
1	2	3	4	5	6

What colors will these numbers be? 9, 12, 13, 26, 27, 100

She then went to answer her questions.

These games are ways for children to play around with numbers and the concepts they are learning. Sometimes I make this a bit more structured and ask them to create a game in a group.

My fourth-, fifth-, and sixth-grade children worked in groups for the following problem. They were creating games.

> This game was invented by _____. The name of our game is _____.
>
> List all of the mathematical concepts used in your game.
>
> What do players need in order to play this game? (What materials are used?)
>
> How is the game played? Write very detailed instructions.
>
> What makes the game challenging?
>
> How can the game be changed to be more challenging to the players? In other words, write some alternatives to the game for those who might play it.
>
> Play the game a few times and see if there are any "bugs" in the game, that is, anything you need to fix in your directions.
>
> What did you change? What is the purpose of your game?

I wanted them to think about how their game went as they played it and what problems arose as they played. They looked closely at how challenging the games were and noticed how challenging games made by other groups were.

> Was your game challenging to you? Why, or why not? What made it challenging?
>
> How did your group work together? How could your group have worked better together?
>
> Whose game did you play? Describe their game challenging to you? Why, or why not?

Cory wrote about how her group worked: "We didn't argue over who went first; instead we rolled the die to see who went first."

At times I need to back off and trust what my students are doing. I'll never forget the time I saw a group of kids who were notorious for not always doing what they were supposed to be doing, playing around with the 3-D base 10 pieces. I saw them building towers and structures, laughing loudly after the towers had fallen.

"OK, you three, this is math workshop! That doesn't mean you sit around and just build stuff!" I said in my sternest teacher voice.

"Oh, no! Jill, this is cool." said Jesse enthusiastically. "The first person who makes the tower fall, has to add up all the pieces." He was so excited and it seemed legitimate. I stepped back and watched. It really was a pretty good game. After the tower fell, the whole group ended up adding the numbers together. What I saw was actually a wonderful collaborative activity. That game became a popular one in the years that followed, and like all games, it had its variations. I learned to ask first before jumping to conclusions.

Kyle and Dave invented a variation of the building game by using pattern blocks. Each pattern block became a different value, and the first one to make the tower fall had to count up the pieces. From that variation came others as well. Here are a few:

- The pattern blocks became fractions of whole numbers.
- The pattern blocks needed to be doubled or halved depending on the color of the block.
- Each person had his own tower rather than there being a group tower.
- The tower closest to a specific number won.

With this particular building game, the kids were beginning to discover how multiplication was connected to addition.

"Megan, why do you have your pattern blocks in those color groups?" I asked as she was beginning to add up her tower.

"Oh, well, my tower fell and I need to add up my blocks. It's easier to put them in groups, like all the reds and all the blues. Then I can add those up faster."

"What makes it faster to add, do you think?"

"Well, I know 5's really well. Like, if I have four blues, and a blue is worth 5, I know that's 20. It's like 5×4. If it's a hard number like 7, I can do this." She pointed to her paper. This is how Megan multiplies numbers she doesn't know:

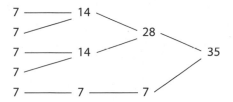

"Can you think of other times it may be important to put numbers in groups like that to make it easier to add?" I asked.

"Well, like with money. It's easier to put all the dimes and nickels and stuff together and then either times them or add them up," she told me.

The more kids get a chance to play with and experiment with numbers, concepts, and skills, the less they fear learning more complex concepts and the more confident they are in developing theories.

As I watched my fourth-, fifth-, and sixth-grade students, this fear or reluctance became apparent. The nice thing about having the same kids for four years in a row is that you know exactly what experiences they have had. I knew the types of mathematical experiences most of my fourth graders had had in the past. Many of the fifth and sixth graders I had taught in their earlier grades, so I knew what their experiences had been in those grades. But

I was constantly surprised by the fearlessness of my fourth-grade students during math workshop. These kids were working on problems that I found to be extremely difficult and concepts not normally introduced in the fourth grade. I discovered how comfortable they were with experimenting with new ideas—fearless—whereas I noticed my oldest children were very reluctant. Many of them had stopped using manipulatives in fourth grade and thought they were "babyish." They wanted to just be told how to do something. So, even though all the fourth graders could not do all the problems accurately, they were much more willing to take risks. They were much more successful at talking about the strategies they were using, and they more often could express their confusion. The older kids were more apt to write a solution without checking to see if it made sense.

Much of this hesitation from the older kids developed because somewhere down the road they had gotten the message that play in math was reserved for the younger grades. It was much easier for the younger kids to come up with creative games to play, for instance. My older kids were not like this throughout the year either; they just needed reassurance from me and their classmates that it was OK to play. Toward the end of the year, they were more comfortable sharing their work and coming up with more creative solutions to problems.

It's important that all levels of learners be given time to play with what they are learning. I know when I am learning something new it helps me if I can practice and play around with what I am learning. I still need to use manipulatives when I'm learning new concepts in math. Aisha teaches me new ideas using a variety of methods. Manipulatives should not only be associated with young children. For instance, Aisha was teaching a lesson on decimals by using the tens strips. It was so much easier for the kids to see how decimals are part of a base 10 system by using the pieces. She gave all the kids a set of base 10 pieces and some small problems to think about, such as "If the hundreds mat is now worth 1, what is the tens strip worth?" I would often see the older kids get the pieces on their own to work on some more complex decimal problems.

Independence and Challenge

Play has various meanings for me. Besides mathematical thinking, play can also show how a child approaches a problem. Independent challenges offer a wonderful stage for play in this way. The children often write how they have challenged themselves during math workshop. These are times when I can observe how a child is challenging herself and what she considers to be a challenge. Kathryn, a first grader at the time, decided that arrays were new to her and that drawing them were a challenge to her. She chose to spend the time creating arrays. Carly, on the other hand, decided to write a problem and solve it:

You have 400 dollars and you want to buy a house. Now here are the rules. You can't spend over 400$. Here are all the prices of the items that you want to buy: couch 30$, bed 20$. Oh yeah, the reason the prices are so low is because you are getting them at a garage sale: table 10$, lamp 5$, mirror 2$.

Try to get as close as you can to 400$. Now, that 400$ is only for the stuff that stays in the house. It is 350$ an acre, and there are 10 acres of land and the house is 1050$. I want to know how much money you spend.

As to why this was a challenge for her, Carly wrote, "Because I have never made up my own problem like this before, and usually when you do something for the first time it is challenging."

As in any classroom of 27 children, there are several levels of understanding. I don't think having a multiage class adds to them. I believe *all* children should be given the opportunity to progress at their own rate of learning. It seems to be accepted that teachers attend more to individual levels of learning in multiage classes than in one-grade classes. But it is important to do this with any class. I often have younger students who are much more experienced mathematically than an older student. Age doesn't define a young learner. Just because I have a student who is in first grade doesn't mean I should expect that child to know how to add to 20. It also doesn't make sense to hold children back from challenging themselves.

I don't track my students by putting them into ability groups. All the children work on the same problems and activities and do them at their own levels of understanding. I don't adjust the problem to fit the child; I let the child adjust the problem to fit her own learning style by choosing her own methods and strategies. Some teachers believe that I do this because I teach a multiage class, but I would teach this way no matter what type of class I had. Yes, there was a very wide span of learning levels in my multiage class, but there would be the same span even if I had a class of eight-year-olds all born on the same day. Individualizing instruction is important for *all* classes, not just multiage classes. Math workshop is a perfect time to let each individual learn at her own pace. One way I foster this individuality is to give my students the chance to challenge themselves during the workshop time. The games and activities the kids undertake reinforce this belief.

One of the activities my kids have done year after year is one with pattern blocks. Each pattern block shape is drawn on the top of a piece of paper. (I have blank sheets like this for the kids to use.) They assign numbers to each shape or ask me to do this for them if they are unsure of how to do it at first. From there, they create designs with the blocks. If they can, they draw the design on the paper and then add up the design elements based on the value of each pattern block. It is easy to see the difference in mathematical experience between the two examples in Figure 4.1 and 4.2. Both of these were challenging to the children who did them. The ages of these kids are not important; what is important is whether they challenged themselves.

Figure 4.1

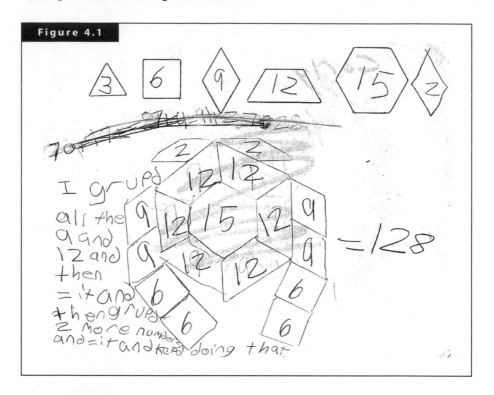

I gruped all the 9 and 12 and then = it and then 9 next 2 more numbers and = it and kep doing that.

= 128

Figure 4.2

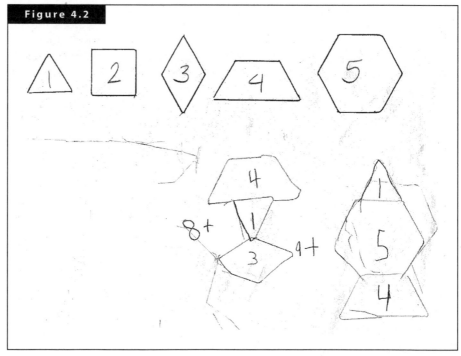

By knowing where each child is on his own learning continuum, I can create problems or activities for him to do during the workshop. For example, the whole class might be working on the same exploration activity, but each child is exploring at his own level. I often ask children to explore numbers. One such activity asked each child to explore a different number. He was to do as much with that number as he could think of. My intent with this particular exploration was to see how each child approached this assignment, how much he could come up with to explain his number. I assigned Dave the number 482 (Figure 4.3) and Kathryn the number 8 (Figure 4.4). These children were at very different places in their mathematical development, yet they could explore their numbers at their own levels.

Often I write a generic problem and assign different numbers or aspects of the problem to each child. For instance, when I asked the kids to explore the visual models for numbers using base 10 pieces, I gave Carly three numbers to draw in base 10, but I also asked her to go further and draw the same numbers using base 5 (Figure 4.5). Because I knew where she was in her development, I could ask her to do this. Some other child, like Kathryn, I may have only given one or two smaller numbers and only to show in base 10 (Figure 4.6). Because Carly knows that she is free to challenge herself,

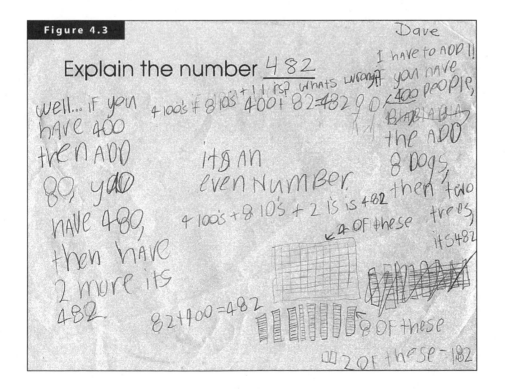

Figure 4.3

Figure 4.4

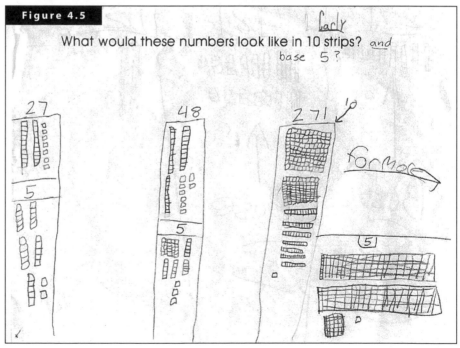

Figure 4.5

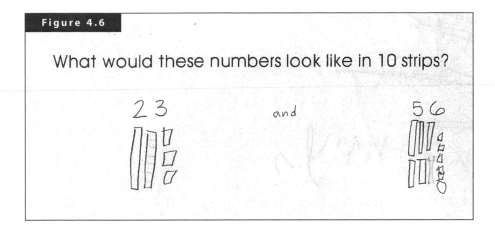

Figure 4.6

What would these numbers look like in 10 strips?

23   and   56

she turned her paper over and drew what she imagined those numbers would look like using base 3 pieces.

Calendar and math workshop are the places where the foundation of mathematics is built. Math workshop is a time for kids to explore and learn new concepts and a place where challenge is not only encouraged but expected. Challenge and independence are fundamental in my classroom. By accepting challenges from me, the kids learn to challenge themselves not only because I ask them to but do so independently, naturally. Challenging oneself becomes an intrinsic part of the learning process.

Integrating It All

Classroom activities should provide students the opportunity to work both individually and in small- and large-group arrangements. The arrangement should be determined by the instructional goals as well as the nature of the activity....

Projects and small-group work can empower students to become more independent in their own learning. Whole-class discussions require students to synthesize, critique, and summarize strategies, ideas, or conjectures that are products of individual and group work.

—*NCTM Curriculum Standards*

What's our big project for this year, Jill?" I hear this question every year just as winter is ending. Each spring we plan a big project that relates to what we are studying, which occupies the kids for a month or more. These projects serve as the culmination of a study we have done and as the culmination of a year of mathematical thinking. All the skills, concepts, problems, explorations, and presentations we have worked on throughout the year are consolidated into a large project that is packed full of problems to solve.

The ideas for the projects initially come from the kids, but the structure of these projects has had a very specific evolution. In my book *A Room with a Different View*, I wrote about the Garden Problem. This two-dimensional problem began the transition into the larger building-type projects we do now. The Garden Problem was challenging, yet since then, I have learned to challenge my students even more. Every year, my students amaze me with what they are able to do, and I push myself to give them more.

Integrating math, science, art, music, reading, writing, social studies, and geography into these large projects is important. When we were studying the Civil War, for example, I wrote a project that focused on helping a group of slaves escape to the North via the Underground Railroad. One mathematical portion of that project dealt with distance and time. We had done some work earlier in the year that focused on distance and time, and in this project the kids could relate that work to the content they were studying.

Throughout the year we work on all the required concepts. These large projects are a way of bringing together as many of those concepts as possible while also making sure that the projects are meaningful, fun, and challenging.

Chapter 5 describes three specific projects from three different years. I like having the kids do a project every year that involves design and building, but I don't like doing the same thing every year. Although each of these are design and building projects, they all grew from different places. The first, Schools of the Future, comes from our year of being time travelers. Hide a Family came from our study of the 1940s. And Design a House was done during the year I taught fourth, fifth, and sixth graders and came out of their interest in design.

More Than Math: Three Big Projects

Project 1: Schools of the Future

"We could start at the island, find this time machine, and travel back in time to other places. Like, we could go back to the Civil War time and stuff like that." That statement came from Dave in June at the end of our year on the island. That year our room had been transformed into an island, and we spent the year working on projects that grew out of that idea (see my book *A Room with a Different View*).

Dave knows more about the Civil War then any other human being I've met, and I thought it would be great to have him be the expert on a study of the Civil War the following year. The kids know how I like to have a year-long focus, and the time travel machine was just right for that.

That next September we became time travelers, and the kids voted on where they wanted to travel. They decided on 1863 Virginia (out of respect for Dave's interest), present-day Arctic, space, and the future. Our study of the Civil War extended from September until winter break, so we had to cut out one place. The kids voted not to go to space, so we studied the Arctic and the future for the rest of that year.

We built a time travel machine that remained in the room all year. It was made out of black crepe paper and carpet roll tubes. We arranged our furniture inside it throughout the year. When we were deciding on what future year to go to, the kids and I sat inside the time machine and discussed it.

"So, we need to leave the Arctic now and continue on into the future," I said. "Where do you want to go? Or, I should say, *to when!*"

"How about the year nine billion?" someone shouted.

"That's dumb," said Chris.

"How come that's dumb, Chris?" I asked.

"'Cause it's too far away," he said.

"How about 2126?" Kyle said quietly.

"OK, why 2126, Kyle?" What a funny date, I thought.

"Because it's as far ahead as we went back. Like, 1863 was 131 years ago, and 2126 is 131 years ahead," he said.

"Cool! I like that idea, don't you?" I asked the class. And that is how we came to travel to the year 2126.

During the study, the kids transformed the room into the year 2126 (or what they imagined that year would look like). It was fun studying this after the Civil War and the Arctic. Their ideas on how to create the environment were imaginative. They made fax machines for the tables, picture phones around the room, a transport machine, and signs that read *There is no racism in 2126*. They transferred what they had learned during the Civil War and decided that in the future there wouldn't be any racism or violence.

As we were working on this topic, we had a lot of questions. The kids were curious about what things would look like 131 years into the future. They wanted to know what cars would be like, if we could fly to the moon, what houses would be like, and most interesting to me, what schools would be like in the year 2126. From that inquiry came the Schools of the Future project, in which the kids built schools for the year 2126 out of wood and posterboard.

■ Design a School for the Year 2126

You and your partner will be designing a school for the year 2126. Your school will need to include a design for one classroom, a gym, and a lunchroom. Your design will need to have one extra room of your choice.

The total area you get for your design will be 1200 square units. (You will be using inches for your plans.) You can divide the 1200 square inches up any way you and your partner decide.

You will be following an order of how to design your school:

1. Draw a *very* rough draft of what your school will look like.
2. Decide what your extra room will be.
3. Figure out how many square inches each room will be.
4. Use the squares to figure out the shape your rooms will be, and glue them onto the large graph paper.
5. Write down the area and the perimeter of each room. Don't forget to write *square units* next to each area and *linear units* next to each perimeter.

	Area	Perimeter
Classroom	_____	_____
Gym	_____	_____
Lunchroom	_____	_____
Extra room	_____	_____

Now draw your blueprints. You need to use a ruler and very carefully transfer your drawing onto white paper. This will be your final paper blueprint, so it really needs to be neat. Straight and neat lines!

Now choose the two rooms you want to build. What will they be?

Next, count how many corners you have in each of those rooms:

    Room 1 =
    Room 2 =
    Total   = _____

OK, now you're ready for your corner pieces.

The walls will be 5 inches tall. Take the total you wrote down for the number of corners. Multiply that number by 5, and that will be how many inches of wood you need to ask for to build the corners of the walls.

Before you come and get your wood … the wood will cost you $3 per 5 inches. So how much money will you be spending on the corner pieces?

Make marks every 5 inches before you cut the wood. You should have exactly the right amount. After you have cut your wood, write C on each piece so you know it is a corner piece.

Now you'll need to make the length pieces.

Write down the lengths of each wall for the two rooms you are building. Remember, we used centimeters, not inches.

   Room 1   Room 2

    Total for room 1 =   Total for room 2 =

    Total for both rooms =

This time the wood will cost you $5 for every 20 centimeters. How much money will you be spending on length pieces?

Write the measurements for cutting on each piece of wood, and cut the pieces.

Next, build the walls. Your walls will be 5 inches high and the same length as the wood lengths you cut. So each wall will be a 5 X ? rectangle (unless of course you have circular walls). We will work together on these measurements.

Your walls will cost you $8 per sheet. How much did you spend on the walls?

Put the walls together. You will need a small cup of wood glue, Q-tips, and index card triangles. You need one triangle for each corner, front, and back, of each wall. What is the total number of triangles you need?

The glue costs $2 a cup. The Q-tip cost 10 cents each. The triangles cost 25 cents each. What are your total costs for the walls?

Project 2: Hide a Family

One year, the kids wanted to transform our room into a town. We called it Kidsville. After the winter break, the kids decided they wanted to do another historical journey. (Since we studied the Civil War, the kids have been interested in other time periods.) Christopher was very interested in Pearl Harbor and all the ships and aircraft of that era. We discussed his interest as a class, and we decided to study the 1940s. Because of the sensitive subjects of that time in history, we approached the war in Europe slowly. We began the study by changing our town into 1942 Kidsville and learning about the home front during the 1940s. From there, it was a natural progression into learning about Europe and the causes of the war.

The kids were intrigued to learn that many European individuals and families had been hidden in the homes of others during the war, so I wrote the Hide a Family project. Actually, before I wrote it, I talked to the kids about it. They had been asking me about the big project for that year. The idea of hiding a family came from their questions, and I wanted to discuss it with them before sitting down to write. This was one of those conversations that touches you so much you know you'll never forget it.

"I was thinking about our big project and I have an idea that I want to talk over with you," I said. "I was thinking we could make houses with secret rooms. What do you think?"

"Cool! Like we could build houses that have a secret room that hid out Jews during the war? Like Anne Frank?" Mary asked.

"Yes, like that," I said.

"Could we put the secret room anywhere we wanted?" asked Shanti.

"Sure, and we'll talk about where a good place would be. We'll have to do some research about how the secret rooms were used in Europe," I added.

"How come only Europe? I was thinking of hiding a Japanese-American family. Could I do that?" Kyle asked. I was speechless. We had been learning and discussing Japanese internment during the war, but I had never mentioned anything about Japanese-Americans being protected like that. Frankly, I don't think I've ever read any information supporting this. Yet Kyle had thought about it and was confused by the fact that Americans didn't hide Japanese-Americans from being sent to internment camps. So even though I doubt there is anything on record about this, I was not only pleased by Kyle's question but touched by his ability and willingness to sympathize with another persecuted group.

"Yes, of course, Kyle. What a wonderful idea. I really don't believe this happened, but I think it's great that you thought of it." This is why I love working with children. I never would have thought of that. Connections like this also reaffirm my strong belief that young children not only *can* learn about historical information but *should*.

"How come Japanese-Americans didn't go into hiding in other people's houses?" Mary asked. It was a question I couldn't answer. From this discussion, I was able to use what the kids had talked about to write the project. The kids built houses that included a secret room. They made these from materials they chose.

■ Hide a Family in 1942!

You and your partner will help hide a family in a part of your home. You may choose a Japanese-American or a European family to hide and help. You need to describe the family you will help. How many people are in the family? Why do they need your help?

You will be designing a home in which you will add a secret room for your family to live in until the war is over. How will you help to hide your family? What will your help mean to the family?

Write a family profile.

Family name:

Nationality of family:

What country does the family live in?

The members of the family are

Write a brief description of the family:

Design the home. Where do you live? Describe your home. Draw a plan of your idea. (Use small graph paper first and then transfer to large graph paper.)

You will need to design and then build the home you live in plus the secret room in which your family will be living until the war ends. The home will need to be very strong and well built.

Your home will need to have at least eight rooms not including the secret room. One-quarter (1/4) of the rooms will be bedrooms. Two-eighths (2/8) of the rooms will be bathrooms. You also need a kitchen and a living room. The remaining rooms can be of your choice.

You need to have some walls in your home that are at 90° angles and some that are at 45° angles.

Design the secret room. It should come off one of the walls that are at a 45° angle.

The walls in the secret room should all be at 90° angles. The secret room must be totally hidden inside your home.

You need to figure out a way to hide the door leading into the secret room from your home. The secret room needs to have a place to keep food, a bathroom, and a bedroom.

Here is a building checklist.

To Do	Done
Small graph paper plan	_____
Large graph paper plan	_____

Check the fractions for the rooms   _____
Check the angles of the walls   _____
Choose materials to build   _____
Begin building   _____
Building complete   _____
Paint   _____
Decorate and furnish   _____
Dolls   _____
Story or poem   _____
Presentation   _____

Decorate and furnish your home. You can paint or wallpaper your walls.

After you have made all the furniture for your home—beds, couches, tables, chairs, and shelves—you count up all the items.

Divide the furniture up in order to give the family you are hiding some furniture. Give the family 1/4 of the silverware and dishes you own. How many did you give away? How many do you have left?

Make a large radio for your living room. It's 1942; sorry, no TV!

Project 3: Design a House

The year I taught a combined fourth, fifth, and sixth grade, my students were very interested in architecture and design. They had noticed a house built out of foam board in one of the upper-grade classrooms. "Let's build houses like that this year, Jill," Dave said after he had seen the house. I asked the teacher about the house. Apparently, it was done by a professional architect. The walls were put together with straight pins pushed into the foam board. We could do that, I thought.

We weren't studying houses or architecture, so I thought we could get to the building of the houses backward that year. Instead of the project coming out of what we were studying, we would study what we wanted to build. I bought a book of house plans from a building supply store. Each student chose a page from the house plan book to have for the first phase of the project.

"Look over your plan, and before we do anything, just discuss what you notice with each other. We'll meet to talk about it together in about 15 minutes," I told them. I walked around and listened in on some of the initial observations.

"I hate that the garage is almost as big as the house," Kim told Rachel and Jamie. "I'd move that if it were my house."

"Where would you put it?" Rachel asked.

"Oh, I'd put it around the side or even in the back. Just so it wasn't sticking out like it is on this plan. You don't notice it so much, but when you see the plan, you can see how big it is and how much room it takes up," Kim said. "Jill, this is cool! I love doing this. I can sit and look at these books for hours. I always make up my own blueprints," she told me.

"Really? I never even knew they had these books. I've never seen them before," I said.

"You're kidding." She looked at me in amazement. When we got back together in the large group, Kim shared her observations about the garage, and other kids shared what they had noticed.

Then they converted their plans into linear and square units. A unit was a quarter inch square, and the kids actually cut out their house plans and glued them onto a piece of quarter inch graph paper. They wrote down the areas and perimeters of each room from the house plan (Figure 5.1).

Enlarging their plans onto white construction paper, they were only to transfer the foundation onto the paper, not the inside walls separating

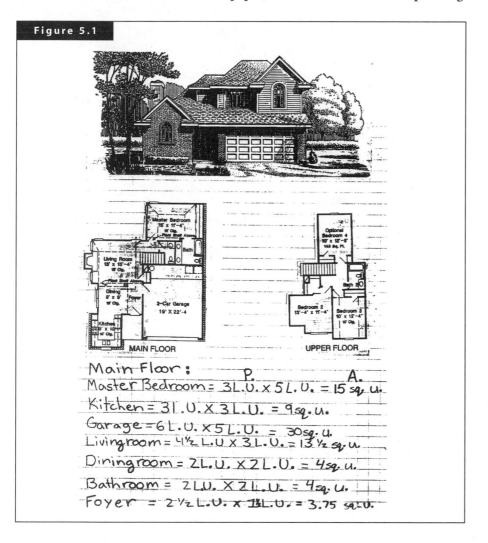

Figure 5.1

rooms. They had a choice of making the plan twice or three times as large, just so they wrote down what they did. They wrote down the new measurements and then began to work on what changes they would make. I wrote up four situations, and out of these, they chose two to work on:

> You have purchased the house, but you don't like the kitchen. It isn't the shape you want or the size you want. Figure out a way to make it bigger, but keep the foundation of the house the same. Make sure you add in the appliances too.

> You have purchased the house, but you don't like the shape of the bedrooms. They either need to be longer or wider. Keep the foundation of the house the same.

> You have purchased the house, but you want to add another small bathroom. You need to figure out where to put it and how it can fit in without changing the foundation of the house.

> You have purchased the house, but you want to add an extra room for an office. You need to figure out where to put it and how it will fit without changing the foundation of the house.

From this practice with looking at plans, foundations, and design, I was able to write the big project of designing and building a house out of foam board.

■ Design a House

Draw the foundation. Your house foundation may not be larger than 12 inches × 12 inches. (It doesn't need to be a square, but it will need to fit inside 12 × 12 square inches.) Remember, you are building this house out of foam board, so if it is too complicated, it may be too hard to build.

Just draw the outline of the base of the house. Don't include the rooms yet. The first draft of your foundation will be done on quarter inch graph paper. Write down the dimensions in square quarter inches and then figure out how many square inches your foundation will be. Write both measurements here:

_____ square quarter inches
_____ square inches

Draw the foundation twice. One will be for the lower level, one for the second floor.

Following the guidelines, *draw in the rooms.* You need to have the following rooms in your house, either upstairs or downstairs:

■ A kitchen that is no larger than 1/4 of the total area
■ A bathroom that is no larger than 1/8 of the total area
■ A living room/dining room/extra room that is no larger than 1/3 of the total area

You also need to have these rooms. Figure out what fraction of the area they take up.

- Bedrooms. Write down how many and how large they are.
- Full bathrooms, which include a shower and bath.

If you want more rooms, make a list of what they are, and write down what fraction of the total foundation they take up.

Now, you should have *your small plan finished* with the total fraction of space each room takes up. Using a pencil and a ruler, *transfer your small plan* onto the larger square inch graph paper. Write the area and perimeter of each room.

If you want to change any requirement for the design of your house you will need to write an explanation as to why you want to change it and how the change will benefit your house.

Advertise your house so it will sell, or show the advertisement you saw that led you to buy your house.

Create an advertisement for your house. It can be an ad in the paper or a brochure. Be sure to include all special features of your house. Include the total square feet and the price of the house. (Use the chart at the end to figure out the price.)

Say where your house is in the world, and show drawings or pictures of that place. Write some text to go with your drawings and pictures. Look at newspaper ads if that helps. Usually these ads are very descriptive. The advertisement should be neat and pleasing to look at.

- Where is your house?
- Where is your house located?
- Is this an urban, rural, or suburban area?
- Is your house on a plain, mountain, hill, or valley?
- Is your house near a river, lake, ocean, streams?
- Describe the setting of your house in detail.

Use this chart as a guide to figuring out the price of your house.

Foundation, not including land	$500 per square unit
Outside walls	$53 per square unit
Floor	$95 per square unit
Ceiling	$29 per square unit
Roof	$48 per square unit
Fireplace	$675
Windows, standard	$150 each
Windows, custom	$265 each
Outside doors	$350 each
Inside doors	$75 each
Toilets	$185 each
Bathtub, standard	$230
Bathtub, large	$430
Sink, bathroom	$85

Sink, utility	$45
Sink, kitchen	$175
Refrigerator	$455
Washer/dryer	$300
Additional appliances	$200 each

Total...so far   _____

Architect's signature:

Cost Auditor's signature:

Communication, brainstorming, sharing, and discussion are the core of these projects. Without collaboration between me and my students, these projects would not have evolved the way they did.

Brainstorming, Sharing, Decisions

One of the first decisions to be made was how to group the kids. We work in groups, as partners, and independently. Sometimes I let the kids choose their own partners, sometimes I ask them to choose someone who is a different age or gender than themselves, and sometimes I choose for them. For the Schools of the Future project, I wanted the kids to work as partners. I put the kids in pairs according to who I thought would work well together on this challenging problem. I did not put more experienced children with less experienced children; I didn't want one partner doing more of the work. Instead, I just chose children who I thought would work well in their partnership. I was curious about how certain kids would work with each other for this project, and that turned out to be a good decision.

For the Hide a Family project, Kyle had the idea to work in groups of three. We voted, and the majority of the class wanted to do this. I had my doubts about groups of three, but I went with their wishes. As it turned out, Kyle said he would rather have worked as partners. It was difficult getting all three members to help out. On the other hand, some of the groups worked better in threes. It all depended on the mix of the kids, but it was a nice idea that the kids wanted to try, and I went with it. I usually don't have the kids work in threes for a big project, because it always seems like one person is either left out or doesn't pull her weight. There was some of that during this project, but not as much as I had expected.

For the Design a House project, the older kids wanted to work alone. That was fine with me, although with 27 houses, the classroom was a disaster area for a long time. It was hard finding room to work, and we used every inch of space, including closets and hallways.

Space became an issue with one part of the Schools of the Future too. I had decided that the total area of the schools would need to be 1200 square units. (When thinking about the design of this problem, I decided they would create four rooms, so 1200 was a number that was easy to divide up. That assumption proved unnecessary, since every partnership used that number in a different way. And they only actually built two of those rooms.) We had spent a good part of the year working on area and perimeter, and with this project, because of the large number, the kids needed to have a space large enough to manipulate schools of 1200 square inches. I called a parent who loves doing work like this and told her I wanted 15 plastic bags, each filled with 1200 square inch pieces. She thought I was nuts, but she did this for me over spring break. It was a life saver because I never would have taken the time to cut all the squares, and it proved to be a great experience for the kids.

When the kids returned from break, I had my 15 plastic bags, each holding 1200 square inch pieces of construction paper. But where on earth could a class of 27 spread out four sheets of large chart paper and 1200 squares? Our lunchroom seemed like a good place. We knew we would have to leave by 10:30 A.M. because that's when they began setting up for lunch. So every morning from 9 to 10:15 we went into our lunchroom, and the partners spread out their four large 1 inch graph chart paper and 1200 square inch pieces of construction paper and started gluing. When one partnership had finished gluing the squares, the kids calculated the area and perimeter of each of the four rooms of their school. When they had finished doing that, they volunteered to help another partnership glue or count. When all the partnerships had finished gluing, we returned to the classroom to work on the next phase of the project.

We solved many problems together during our daily whole-group discussions. This was true for each project. The sharing sessions were important. The kids asked questions and shared problems or concerns they were having. Through the discussions, we were able to help each other.

Megan brought up her difficulty getting her plan to come out like what she was visualizing in her mind. She discussed her concern during the Schools of the Future project.

"Jill, we want our room to be a half circle, so how do we put the squares down on the graph paper?" Megan asked one morning as she was trying to form her squares on graph paper to be an arc.

"You could just do it like a diagonal," Dave suggested.

"Yeah, but it wouldn't be a circle-looking shape," Megan said.

"Yeah, but that doesn't matter if you know what it should look like, does it, Jill?" Kyle asked.

"I don't know. What do you think?" I directed the question back to Megan.

"I guess that would work, if it's OK."

"Maybe when you transfer this plan to your blueprint, you can make that arc more accurate," I suggested. This worked. When she transferred her plan into a more accurate blueprint drawing, she was able to make the arc.

Sometimes the discussions were not about specific mathematical ideas but about some confusion over the content of the problem. The Hide a

Family project, which was drawn out of a complex topic, brought up many interesting discussions. The first things the groups needed to decide about the family they were going to hide were its name, its nationality, the country it lived in, and who were the family members. They then wrote short descriptions of their families. They also described where they themselves lived and their homes. These were fictional families, and the kids pretended that they were living in Europe or the United States in 1942. After the kids came up with their family profiles, I took the information and made a large chart showing all the data from each group. I hung this chart up on the wall so it would be easy for everyone to see and so we could all refer to each other's families and know where the families were from. I think there were about as many Japanese-American families as there were European ones. The kids knew that they could choose to hide a Jewish family, a Gypsy family, or any other persecuted European group. They wanted to discuss choosing names for their families. They wanted to know types of names usual among European Jews.

They really threw me for a loop when they asked me about Jewish names, and looking back, I wonder if I handled it the right way. The kids who were hiding European Jews asked me for advice; they thought that since I was Jewish, I'd be able to help. "Jill, what are Jewish names?" Caitlin asked me.

"Jewish names? I don't know, you mean like last names?" I stumbled. For some reason, this made me uncomfortable. I didn't want to generalize with names, although growing up in a mostly Jewish neighborhood as a child, I knew there were definite patterns to the names as well as names that were often carried by Jewish families.

"Well, yeah, I figure the first names are pretty much the same, right?" Caitlin said. I felt foolish.

"Well, let me see. I guess I can tell you some names of people who I went to school with. Would that help?" And I proceeded to list names of families that I remembered. "I don't know if that helps or not, but those are a few of the names I remember. It makes me feel a bit funny telling you that because I'd hate for you to think that just because someone has a certain last name, that makes a person one way or another. Do you understand that? You can't assume that just because someone has your last name, that they believe as you do." What a stupid answer, I thought. I'm not sure why this bothered me so much, but it did.

"No, that's OK, we can also look in some of the books," Caitlin said. My answer seemed to confuse only me! But I was glad I had talked about it with the kids. In the end, one of the Jewish families was named Frank after Anne Frank. Most of the kids chose names from stories we had read.

Kyle's group named their Japanese-American family Nomo after the famous baseball player. The kids became connected to the families they were hiding. The project brought a difficult concept a little closer, so they could relate. They began to care for their families and worked hard to help them.

The Design a House project sparked many discussions, and we solved many problems together as a group. Some of the problems were things I had overlooked. One such discussion focused on the measurements of the walls on the blueprint and how they related to those of the actual foam board model. Twelve-year-old Josh had noticed that when he went to attach his 4.5 inch × 8 inch wall to the floor, his wall was no longer 8 inches tall.

"What happened? Why isn't it 8 inches anymore? Did you cut it wrong?" someone asked him.

"No, but when you attach it to the floor, you add on another quarter inch because of the foam board. So now the walls are 8 1/4 inches."

"Hm. What should we do?" I asked.

"It doesn't matter," someone said.

"Would you say that to the builder building your house?" Tessia responded.

"Yeah, I agree with Tessia," I said. "It does matter, but I don't think I understand Josh's problem yet. Can you explain it more?"

"Well, when you measure the wall from the outside, it is more than 8 inches because of the foundation. The floor is a quarter inch thick," he explained.

"Why don't we just make the walls 7 3/4 inches high instead?" Dave suggested. "That way, they'll be 8 inches tall from the outside."

"What do you think?" I asked.

"That was easy," Kim said.

"I see a problem with that. Does anyone else?"

"I do," replied Alex, "If we make the walls 7 3/4 inches tall, then they won't be 8 inches tall when you measure from the inside. The wall, assuming you could stand inside the house, would not be 8 feet." (We were using a scale of 1 inch = 1 foot.)

"That's what I was thinking too," I said.

"So, are 8 foot walls the measurement from the inside or from the bottom of the foundation?" Kim asked. And that set us off measuring the heights of the walls in our classroom and in their homes. They did figure out that the measurements should be made from the floor, not from the bottom of the foundation. This whole topic was something I hadn't thought of, but it meant more to them to work out the problem than for me to tell them what to do.

Some of their problems with their houses were physical!

"My finger is killing me from pressing these pins into foam board!" someone said. To attach the foam board walls together, we used straight pins.

"That happened to me too. Does anyone have a secret for not getting hurt fingers from the pins?" I asked.

"Yeah, I do," Josh said, "I just use the bottom of the X-acto knife. It works pretty well."

"I use the floor. I just push the floor into the pin," Ned said.

"It doesn't hurt if you are using the green stuff. It's easier to push in," Kelly said. We were using two different types of foam board. Some kids thought thimbles would help, and the next day we had a dozen or so thimbles to use.

Mini-Lessons

These projects lent themselves well to mini-lessons, either planned or on the spot. I held group, partnership, and individual mini-lessons. When the large graph paper plans we were working on in the lunchroom were completed for the Schools of the Future, we remained in our classroom to do the rest of the project. The next step was to transfer these large plans onto smaller graph paper. The kids came up with several ways to do this during a class discussion.

"Well, we could just count up each side and then do the same on the little graph paper," offered Carly.

"Yeah, or else we could also measure the sides to make it more accurate," said Dave.

"Except, it's already an inch; we already know it's an inch because of the graph paper, so that would be a wasted step almost," said Tessia.

"Explain to me again how that would be a wasted step," I said. "I understand the large paper is in 1 inch squares, but I don't get what you mean about its being a waste of time."

"OK, well, if you already know that one side is, say, 14 inches, then why measure it?" she said.

"Yeah, but how much do you know to measure on the small paper? Unless it's an inch too. But that would be kind of dumb, to have 1 inch paper again, wouldn't it?" Kyle said.

"Oh, yeah," Tessia said. "I forgot about the smaller graph paper. Well, Jill, what size is it? If it's half an inch, we could just halve it; if it's a quarter inch, we could just divide by 4. Right?"

"And how would you go about doing that? Let's do some practice ones, because I'm not sure what size small graph paper we'll use. Let's try it with half inch first. I'm going to pretend I have a rectangular room that is 16 inches × 4 inches. Here is a large piece of graph paper. Does anyone want to draw that on here for us?" After the rectangle was drawn, we talked about how to transfer it onto half inch graph paper.

"What would you do, Shanti?"

"I'd just cut the number in half," she said.

"What number?" I asked.

"The 16 and the 4," she said.

"So your new perimeter, or dimensions, would be what?"

"8 × 2," she said. And she drew that onto half inch graph paper.

"I wouldn't do it that way," Kyle said. "I'd double it, not halve it because now it's too small. I would do 32 × 8."

"But then it's just the same size. Why can't we just do 16×4 on the smaller graph paper and just change the unit? Like, instead of 16 linear *inches*, it would be 16 linear *quarter inches*," Tessia said.

"Both you and Kyle have excellent points. Let's go back to my rectangle. Instead of trying to change the number, let's change the units of measurement instead. So, if one side is 16 linear inches, how many linear half inches is the side? Take some time to discuss this with your partner, and then we'll share." The kids talked about this among themselves for about ten minutes. Some kids got up and used unifix cubes, some used rulers, some just sat there and figured it out by looking at the graph paper.

"OK, so what did you discover?" I asked.

"It's 32 half inches in 16 inches," Jacob said.

"Yes, we got that too," Kathryn said.

"How did you get 32?" I asked.

"Well, we figured that if there are 2 half inches in 1 inch, and 4 half inches in 2 inches, we just kept doing that and got 32 half inches in 16 inches," Kathryn said.

"We just doubled it," said Jacob.

"Did anyone do it a different way?"

"Yeah, we got out 16 unifix cubes and pretended that they were one inch. Then we split that in half and got 8," said Pat.

"Did anyone else get 8?" No response. "Why didn't you get 8, Kyle?"

"Well, because you wanted to know how many half inches were in 16 inches. What you guys did was to just split 16 in half. But you needed to actually double 16," he said.

"Why?" I asked.

"Because. Well, here, can I use the unifix cubes?" And Kyle proceeded to explain to Pat and the rest of the class what he had done. He took 16 unifix cubes and with a pen showed that there are two halves in one of the cubes. He continued to split the 16 cubes in half with a pen and had Pat count up all the halves. He seemed to have understood what Kyle was explaining to him.

We did more work with half inches, quarter inches, and centimeters during the next few weeks of that problem through mini-lessons and sharing times.

Another mini-lesson during the Schools of the Future came about after we had been looking at real blueprints Ross had brought in from home. We had noticed that the symbols for the doors were quarter circles. This was a perfect time to introduce and practice using compasses.

"Does anyone know what this is?" I asked one morning, holding up a compass.

"Yeah, it's the thing to draw circles," Ross said.

"Do you know what it's called?"

"A compass?" Tessia said, a bit unsure of herself.

"Yes. It's a compass," I responded.

"How come it's called a compass? I thought the thing that tells where you are is a compass," Kyle asked.

"Yeah, they are both called compasses. Does anyone know how to use one of these?" I asked. No one had used one, although many had seen one before. "Let's talk a little about this compass, and then you and your partner can take one and practice making circles, half circles, and quarter circles." The kids went off to practice using compasses. This is a hard thing to do! It's hard to keep the pointy part of the compass so that it doesn't move, but they helped each other and did the best they could. They practiced making circles with a given radius as well, since their doors would have a required radius. The doors needed to have a radius of 3, so they first practiced using the compasses and then, when they were confident, drew on their blueprint.

I introduced protractors during the Hide a Family project. The kids were working on drawing and measuring angles on their houses, and I thought it would be fun to show them what these were used for. I still have a hard time using a protractor, so I thought it would be interesting for me to try and explain it to the kids. With a set of protractors, I held small-group mini-lessons with those children who wanted to learn how to use one. Several kids came to the mini-lesson on protractors, and others decided to figure out other ways to check their angles, and we shared these during one of our daily sharing times.

"Well, I didn't get the protractor, so I just took a piece of paper and knew that the corner of it was 90°. Then I folded it, and since it was half, I knew that was 45°," said Megan.

"Oh, cool. But what if the angles in your house weren't 90° or 45°? Then what did you do?" asked Jacob.

"Well, I just looked at it and if it was closer to 90°, I just chose a number that was not 90 but close to it. If it was closer to 45°, I just chose a number closer to that."

"Megan, what a great way to estimate the angles. Now, why are those *estimations* and not accurate measurements?" I asked.

"Because she just kind of guessed instead of using a protractor," Kyle answered. And that was how we measured the angles. It didn't really matter to me if the angles were accurate. What was important was that the kids could estimate angle measurements that were appropriate. We practiced using Megan's method on other pieces of paper before doing the actual measurements on the plans.

During the Design a House project, besides the large-group mini-lessons I often held small-group mini-lessons on certain parts of the project. Actually, it was often the kids who held these mini-lessons. Josh was the expert on building the stairs. He actually made stairs for some kids in exchange for pins or other needed materials.

I spent a good part of my time during each of these projects having conferences or mini-lessons with individual children. I walked around asking questions and learning what the kids could do and what they needed assistance with. This is the best form of authentic assessment I can do. Through conferences and mini-lessons, I learn the most about my students.

Improvisations

When I teach teachers, I share my problem and project ideas with them but then ask them to think about how they could adapt mine or create their own projects to fit with what they are doing in their classrooms. Projects come from our classroom community: what we are studying and learning at that point in time. But, more important, they are ever-changing even as we work on them. The projects in this chapter went through many changes during the time we worked on them.

There always seems to be a part of the problem that isn't appropriate or doesn't fit, and there are also things that need to be added to the original after we are well into the project itself. This is one of the main reasons I am so cautious about passing out these projects to be used by teachers; they change so much from what is typed on the paper, and there is so much that is not even on paper.

The Schools of the Future had many changes and additions to the original written problem. One change could only have come to my attention as we were in the midst of building the schools. The walls of the schools were being made out of posterboard. The kids measured how tall the walls would be, cut them out, and attached them to the outside of 3/4 inch wooden supports. Because the corners showed the wood, we put on corner pieces. These were strips of posterboard the height of the room but only about an inch wide. The kids bent the piece in the middle and glued it onto the outside corner of the building. This also proved to give an extra bit of strength. One day we talked about the walls.

"Jill, I don't think it looks so good because you can see the wood supports when you're inside the room," Carly said. She was right. Because we put the posterboard on the outside of the wooden structure, the wood was exposed on the inside.

"Hm. You're right. So what do you suggest?"

"Why not put walls on the inside too," she suggested.

"I like that idea. What do you all think?" I asked the class. For the most part, everyone agreed. There was some grumbling about having to do more walls, but we decided to do it anyway. They also made the extra corner pieces for the inside corners. These inside walls really did make the rooms look better.

Also during that project the kids began to think of other things they could add to their schools to make them look more real.

"Jill, wouldn't it be neat if we could put lights in the schools?" someone asked.

"Great idea! We can put lights in. We'll put electricity into the schools." And for the next few weeks we talked about electricity. I picked up the electricity box we had among the science supplies in the school, and the kids played around with batteries, lightbulbs, sockets, and wires.

It was actually easy to add the lights because of the two sets of walls the kids had built. The battery fit somewhat easily between the two walls. The lightbulbs and sockets were a bit large for the rooms, but they looked good anyway.

One part of the Hide a Family project said that some walls in the house would need to be at 90° angles and others would need to be at 45° angles. This is a great example of the kids teaching me the absurdity of my thinking! It is easy to get carried away with wanting to fit specific concepts into a problem, but at times it takes away from the authenticity of the problem.

"Jill, how come these walls need to be at 45°?" asked Chris. "It's not the way we want our walls to be, and it isn't really working."

"Yeah, not for us either. Besides, how many 45° walls do you have in a house anyway?" Megan said.

"You're right. I have no idea why I put that in. Probably because it would be a way for you to focus on angles as you plan and build," I said. "How about instead of making the walls fit the angles, which seems silly now, you measure the angles of your walls *after* you finish your blueprints? Does that sound better?" It did, and that's how they proceeded.

I had also written that the secret room would need to have a place to keep food, a bathroom, and a bedroom. Those requirements also changed as the kids researched just how small the hiding places really were. They learned that the hiding place where Anne Frank lived was actually very spacious compared to others that people lived in during their time in hiding.

I was humbled during the Design a House project when the kids wanted to build roofs.

"It's not in the requirements, and I'm not sure we'll have enough foam board for that," I said, hoping they'd drop the idea. I just didn't feel like getting into roofs.

"I *really* want to build a roof, Jill" said Alex. OK. I told Alex to go off and build a roof and then he could explain how he did it to the rest of us. I was amazed as I watched Alex build his roof. He actually built trusses to support the top. He had an odd-shaped second floor, and the roof he built was really good. He became our roof expert. We also asked kids from the high school architecture class to come and talk to us about types of roofs, and most of the kids chose to build roofs for their houses after that.

I have learned over the years to listen to my kids and not only to accept changing my problems but to expect it.

Materials

The materials for these projects came from many different places. Some years I purchased the materials, and some years I asked for donations.

For the Schools of the Future project I bought square wooden rods. They were strong wood and made good supports for the walls. I spent a lot for this wood, though, and I don't know if I could or would do that again without asking for some help with the cost.

We hadn't worked with this wood before, so we took some time to talk about how to use it for building the rooms.

"How do you think we should start building?" I asked one morning during a group share.

"We could use nails and hammers and stuff," Chris said.

"Does everyone agree? Can you think of a reason why that may or may not work?" I asked.

"I think the wood looks kind of small to use a hammer," said Megan.

"You know what Megan? I was thinking the same thing. It's a great idea, Chris, and I'd love to have you actually use hammers and nails, but for this building, I don't know if it would be the best way to build. So if we can't use nails, how else will we get the walls to stand up?"

"Glue?" Caitlin said.

"Ah, glue. That might work, but how would we make sure it is strong enough?" I asked.

"I think just glue wouldn't work, but remember when we went on the boat trip last year to look at the bridges? We learned by looking under them that triangles were strongest. Could we use triangles to attach the wood together with strong glue?" Kyle said. Kyle had remembered going under some of the bridges on the Willamette River the year before. We were doing a project on making strong bridges, and the kids planned and organized a trip on a river boat so we could look under the bridges. It was a wonderful trip, and they learned that triangles were a common geometric shape used in structures. They hypothesized that triangles must be very strong. So we decided to put the walls together using triangles and strong wood glue.

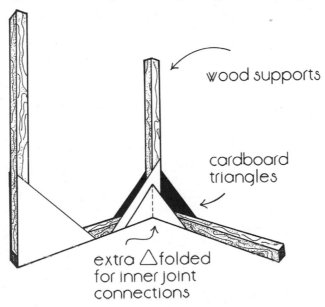

wood supports

cardboard triangles

extra △ folded for inner joint connections

It was hard doing this because the glue was so sticky, but they muddled through, and the skeletons of their schools were complete.

I needed tools. I bought some saws that looked small enough for the kids to use but also strong enough to cut the wood. I asked the kids to bring in small saws if they had them. Before they could cut, they had to do some preliminary work. On completion, the schools would be 5 inches high. Before the kids could make their first cuts, they needed to figure out how many corners each room had. They looked at their blueprints to figure this out. Each corner on their plan would become a support on the building. They circled the corners to get the total number of 5 inch supports they would need. Then I had them take the total number of corners and multiply by 5. For example, if a partnership had eight corners, the kids multiplied 8×5 to get 40, the number of inches they would need to measure out when they came to me for their wood. When they got their wood, they marked it off into 5 inch sections and sawed it.

The saws I bought ended up being all wrong. For some reason I had bought metal saws instead of wood saws. The kids worked hard on the sawing, but it was getting frustrating. So I asked a parent to come in with her electric saw and make the cuts for the kids. Some kids still chose to saw their own.

For the Hide a Family project, I let the kids choose the materials for building their houses. Some of the houses had two floors, and I was curious to see how the kids would build them.

"We want to use those square, long wooden things like we used last year for the schools of the future. Is that OK?" asked Kyle.

"Sure, I think we have some left over. I can maybe buy a half order so it won't be so expensive," I said.

"We want to use a few carpet roll tubes cut in half and posterboard," said Chris.

"Carpet roll tubes? Those are huge!" said Mary. (We used carpet roll tubes often to build structures in the room.)

"No, not the whole one. We want to cut it in half," Chris explained.

"Chris, go get a tube and show us what you mean," I suggested. He brought over a carpet roll tube and showed us what he was thinking. He did figure out that he would actually need a quarter tube rather than a half tube. He told us how the secret room would be behind the toilet.

"The toilet will be up against the tube. Then it will slide out and the family can crawl up the tube."

"So the tube will be part of the house?" I asked.

"Yeah, it'll be what holds the house up," he said. Chris and his group worked so hard on that house. I can't even remember how many times it fell apart, but they were persistent, and in the end it was actually fairly steady.

The year of Design a House, I was flat broke and knew I would not be able to buy a class set of X-acto knives or enough foam board for 27 houses. What to do? I asked the kids how we could get the foam board.

"We could use the money we made harvesting the walnuts," someone said.

"Yeah, I guess we could, but I thought we should save that money for something special. Not that the houses aren't special, but I don't want to use our money on this. What do you think?" Everyone agreed to save that money for something else.

"My dad uses that stuff in his work," Kelly said.

"Really? Cool. Ask him if he could get us some, OK?" I said.

"What about PSS money?" Cory asked. PSS was the parent support group at the school. It often gave small grants to teachers for special projects.

"Great idea, Cory! Let's write a proposal." I ended up writing the proposal myself because I wanted to get it out as soon as I could. We received the money, and I used it to buy foam board, X-acto knives, and straight pins. Kelly's dad also sent in a bundle of foam board, which turned out to be better for some of the kids. It was green foam board that is used in window installation, and it was much easier to push pins into. So the kids actually had a choice between types of foam board. I did end up spending a little of my own money but not nearly as much as I had in the past. I have learned to ask parents to send in what they can.

Invitation to Play

One of my favorite parts of all these projects is watching the kids play. When they were finished building the houses, they pretended they were inside, they imagined what it would be like to live in a small space, they decorated their schools with wacky things, and they had fun. Having fun with what they are learning is an important part of a successful project experience.

Just the idea of creating a school for the year 2126 was invitation enough for play. The kids used their imaginations and knowledge to decorate the rooms the way they wanted to. Paige and Kathryn had a hot tub in their gym. They said that in the future there would be hot tubs in schools. Many kids made round tables in the lunchroom. On a field trip that year to a college, we ate in the cafeteria with round tables. The kids decided the cafeteria would be less noisy and there would be fewer problems if they could sit at smaller round tables. They put up posters, pictures, and kids' work on the walls. I often threw in my own ideas, like wanting all the classrooms to face out onto a beautiful garden where the kids could sit and visit with one another. What a dream.

Even the paint jobs of the schools were unique. Before we painted with color, the kids primed the walls. We talked about priming walls and why that's important. Some of the kids knew about primer from their own houses' being painted. I bought white acrylic paint for the primer. When the primer was dry, the kids looked at color cards and then chose their colors.

The paint jobs were very creative. I think out of 14 there were only a few solid-color schools. The rest were painted in designs and pictures.

With the Hide a Family project, the kids had to create their play within the boundaries of sensitive historical information. The ideas for where to put the secret room were very thoughtful and at times even feasible. Chris's group wanted to put a small trap door behind the toilet. When the toilet moved forward, the little door would open and the family could crawl up into an old unused chimney. Kyle's group put the secret room under the house. Ashley's secret room was behind the fireplace and up the chimney.

Part of the project was to decorate and furnish the houses. We had wallpaper, flooring, and carpet samples, and anything else the kids wanted to bring in to use as decoration for their houses. Some kids brought in dollhouse furniture, and I bought Chris's group a dollhouse-sized toilet. (It was an old-fashioned one with a pull string, perfect for the time period.)

The fourth, fifth, and sixth graders were no different from the younger children in their desire to play with their houses. Dave and Alex made little "pin ships" out of scraps of the foam board. They put all of their pins in this little structure and sent it back and forth to one another. Yes, it is appropriate, and even necessary, for ten-, eleven-, and twelve-year-olds to play. When they designed their houses, they projected their imaginations and their desires into them. Some kids included indoor pools, sports centers, and state-of-the-art appliances. Carly had a 10 foot fountain in the middle of her upstairs hall.

Final Steps and Presentations

This last step varies depending upon the project. When every single piece of the project is finished, we decide how we are going to present and display the work. Each year has been different, from formal presentations in class to large exhibit nights.

The first official writing the kids did for Schools of the Future was a description of their schools. They had to write the population of their schools: how many students, how many staff members. They named their schools. Some of the names were The Cool School of Kids and Staff, The School of Progress, and The World's School. I thought the answer to my population inquiry was interesting. The majority of the partnerships had a 1 to 3 ratio of staff to kids, and the total number of students in the school was under 50. They were also asked to describe how their schools were set up. Kyle and Alicia wrote, "There are two teachers in a classroom and there are two classrooms. One of the rooms has kindergartners, first grade, and second grade, and the other classroom has third, fourth, and fifth graders. Sometimes they would write outside."

Dave and Jordan wrote, "There are five rooms: two classrooms, one library, one lunchroom, one gym. Each class goes to each room and stays there an hour. There are mixed grades. It goes from kindergarten to eighth grade."

Philosophy statements were written next. We discussed what we value in our schools and what we wanted to advertise to the public about those beliefs. The following are some of the philosophy statements the partnerships wrote about their schools. Dave and Jordan wrote, "There are nice kids, they learn doing things rather than using worksheets. It is a public school, and the staff is nice."

Kyle and Alicia wrote, "There is no principal, and sometimes the teacher would act like one of the kids. And help one of the kids if they needed help. And sometimes the teacher would let the kids be independent."

Tessia and Melissa wrote, "The School of Progress works together like a community. They go to PE together and learn from each other. They respect each other and the staff like a community."

Reading these philosophy statements confirmed my feeling that these kids could teach administrators and teachers a lot about how schools should and could be.

The final step in this project was to present the schools to the rest of the class. The partnerships were not supposed to just stand up and present the school to us, they were to convince us that their school was worth going to. We, the rest of the class, pretended to be an audience of prospective parents. The kids were to convince us to send our children to their school. They took a few days preparing for their presentation. Some did skits, others made posters, and others just talked about their schools. They needed to present their blueprints, buildings, and complete descriptions of their school, including the philosophy statement. They also needed to figure out a way to display all parts of their presentation in a neat, organized way (see, for example, Figure 5.2).

When we had completed the entire project, I made books for the kids that described all the steps in this long project. Since they had worked so hard on it, I thought they should have a memento of everything that went into it. I took three photographs of each child holding up one piece of the problem: the large graph paper with the 1200 square units, the floor plan, and the blueprint. I also took a photograph of one of their rooms. When the photographs came back, I glued them to a piece of paper with the statement "This is a picture of. . . ." The kids wrote about the pictures (Figure 5.3).

Also included in this little book were a few questions I asked the kids to answer. One question was, What was the hardest part of this whole problem for you? The responses ranged from gluing the wood together to working with a difficult partner. I also asked, What did you do to solve that even though it was so hard for you? Kyle wrote about the gluing being hard: "I just put the stick face down and when I put the other stick on I pushed a little harder and it stuck." The last question was, What are all the things you learned by doing this project? Kyle wrote, "How to use primer paint, elec-

Figure 5.2

tricity, centimeters, and compasses. And it's going to take hard work to be a architect."

In the front of the books I put a list of all the steps it took to do this problem (Figure 5.4). The kids and I sat together one day and listed all the steps in order. It took up two and a half pages, but it was fun going through the problem this way.

When all of the books had been put together and the presentations finished, we put out schools, blueprints, floor plans, description and philosophy statements, and books on display for the parents to view.

The end of the Hide a Family project was a bit different. There was no formal presentation in class. We decided to take all we had learned during the months we had studied the 1940s and put it on display in an exhibition that parents were invited to attend at night. We decided we needed a lot of room to show all the work we had done, so we reserved the school's multi-purpose room for a night. The Hide a Family project was set up on large lunchroom tables. Next to each house were the descriptions of the families, the photographs they had drawn, the plans and blueprints, and a copy of the project requirements. Besides the Hide a Family project, the kids' written research was on display: our Anne Frank poems, home front game boards the kids created, various pieces of writing, ration books, and problems for

Figure 5.3

This is a picture of... Paige
then We DiD
BLue Prints
Prints are Blue things
that first you Do Lines
with Pensil then you
trase it over with Blue
PensiL

the parents to solve that the kids had solved during the study. We displayed all the books we read along with books we had used in our research. It was a wonderful night and a great way for the kids to share their work with their parents (Figure 5.5). Their assessment was sharing with their parents what they had learned about the 1940s and World War II.

The Design a House project ended with the kids needing to figure out how much money they had spent on their houses and furnishings (Figure 5.6). I gave them prices for materials, everything from the foundation to the window coverings. They had to calculate the amount of wood used, square

Figure 5.4

Here are the steps of the problem

We made drafts of what we wanted our schools to look like.

We were to design four rooms of our school: a classroom, a gym, a lunchroom, and an extra room of our choice.

We grouped 1200 square units into groups. (Most of us did 100's, but some did 20's and 10's.)

We decided on the area of each of our four rooms.

We spent a long time gluing the square units onto large graph paper.

We wrote down the area and perimeter of each room on the large graph paper.

We transferred the large graph paper plans onto small graph paper by using half of the perimeter of the large graph paper.

We made floor plans of the four rooms we designed.

We made blueprints by using half the measurements of the large plans.

We used rulers to keep the lines very straight. Some of us used L- and T-shaped rulers.

We used compasses to make the doors and rulers for the windows. (The doors had a radius of 3 inches, and the windows were 4 inches long.)

We went over our pencil drawings with a blue pencil.

We began to build our schools. We had to choose only two rooms.

We counted our corner pieces and multiplied by 2.

We cut our wood for the supports of the school. They needed to be 5 inches tall. We had to multiply the number of corners we added up by 5 and go get our wood. Then we measured off 5 inches on the long wood and sawed.

We wrote C on all those pieces so we wouldn't forget they were corner pieces.

We measured out the length pieces of the rooms in centimeters. (We used centimeters because we thought it would be more accurate than inches. But it was kind of a pain switching from inches to centimeters.)

We had our numbers, and someone else cut out wood for us because the saws were really hard to use.

We got triangles and wood glue and began to put the walls together. We used triangles because that makes the walls very strong.

After the walls were complete, we put the walls together.

We cut out posterboard to the size of each wall and glued it to the outside of the wooden frames.

We put on posterboard corner pieces to make it even stronger.

We decided to put in inside walls as well.

We put on a posterboard floor.

We primed the outside and inside walls with white primer.

We chose our colors from a color strip and painted the walls and trim.

We put in electricity. We experimented with batteries and wire and lightbulbs. We tried to put the wires in between the outside and inside walls but the batteries were kind of fat.

We added flooring (carpet, tile, linoleum).

We made things to go inside.

We wrote descriptions about our schools. We had to write the population: how many students and staff were in our schools, and we wrote school philosophies.

We drew pencil maps of our schools.

We worked on presenting our schools to each other. We had to persuade other people to send their kids to our school.

We presented our schools to the class.

We wrote about pictures that Jill took of us holding parts of the problem.

We wrote about what we thought the hardest part was.

We wrote about what we learned doing this whole problem/project.

We showed our displays to our parents.

Figure 5.5

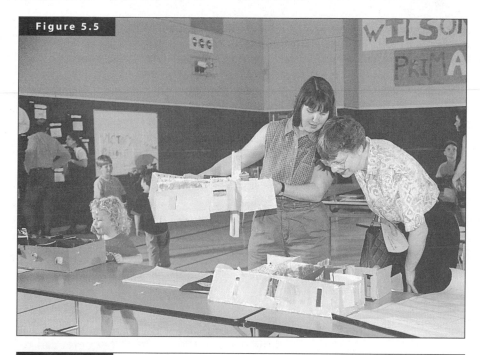

Figure 5.6

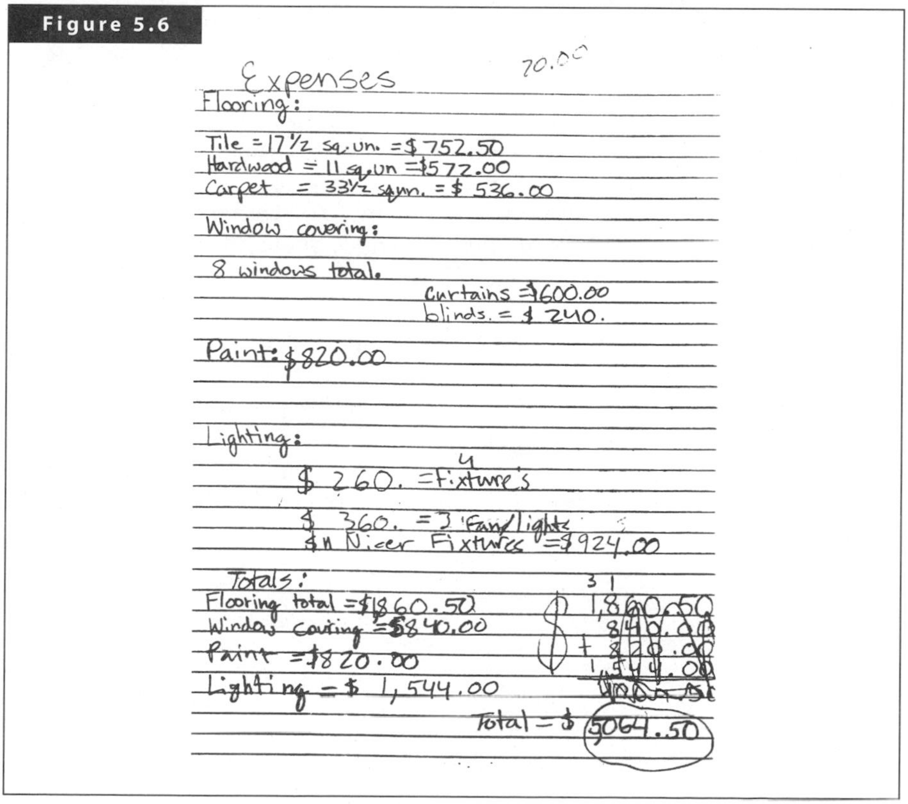

Expenses   70.00

Flooring:

Tile = 17½ sq. un. = $752.50
Hardwood = 11 sq. un = $572.00
Carpet = 33½ sq.un. = $536.00

Window covering:

8 windows total.

        Curtains = $600.00
        blinds. = $ 240.

Paint: $820.00

Lighting:
              4
    $ 260. = Fixtures
    $ 360. = 3 Fan/lights
    $4 Nicer Fixtures = $924.00

Totals: 3 1
Flooring total = $1860.50 $ 1,860.50
Window covering = $840.00   + 840.00
Paint = $820.00   + 820.00
Lighting = $ 1,544.00   1,544.00

             Total = $ (5064.50)

footage of carpet used, and prices of windows. They were surprised to see just how expensive their houses were.

After they had turned in these budget sheets, I gave them another sheet that showed the amount they had gone over budget and would need to cut. This was frustrating for the kids. Dave came up to me one afternoon whining, "Gee, Jill, now all I can have in my house is shades." Most of the kids had to cut down from their original purchases, but I asked some to add more. Michael thought he had pulled a fast one by purchasing the least expensive items and not putting in certain things like carpet or wood floors. He said he could just use the concrete slab for his floor. It was easier to say that than to add up all the large numbers. So, when I gave him his new budget sheet, I wrote a limit he needed to exceed. For the ending, we shared the houses, plans, and budgets with each other.

What I Learn

After doing such elaborate and challenging problems with children, I am constantly amazed by what my students are capable of. They never fail to exceed my expectations. This reaffirms my belief that young children can handle challenging things that we usually save for older children. For instance, using compasses is not usually introduced in early primary grades, yet it is something that they can understand and use. After the Schools of the Future project, and for long afterwards, kids would often ask to use compasses when they were drawing circles or arcs.

Mathematically the children surpassed my expectations, but they also surprised me by what they knew and wanted for their learning. What they wrote in their philosophy statements taught me much about what they wanted in a school. Wanting to include Japanese-Americans in their quest to hide a family from the atrocities of war taught me just how empathetic a child can be when exposed to injustices in the world. Kids can be presented with topics we usually think of as not appropriate for them, and kids can do things we usually think they aren't ready for. If we listen to our students, let them show us just what they are capable of, we learn a whole lot more than where a curriculum guide ends. Sometimes we need to *teach* less and let kids *learn* more.

Show Me What You Know

Assessment should reflect what we understand about how students learn mathematics. Learning is an active social process in which students construct their mathematical knowledge from experience. This process is individual—no two students "learn" exactly the same thing from the same activity. Learning takes time—different students require different amounts of time and experience. Learning is not linear. With this view of learning, the essential assessment question becomes, "Where are these students in the process of making sense of the mathematics?" rather than "Which students have acquired concept X or skill Y?"

—*NCTM Assessment Standards*

How do I know what my kids know and have learned if I don't give them math tests? I let them *show* me what they know and what they have learned. A standardized test, for instance, shows me how my children approach testing, not what they are being tested on. I already know what my students can and can't do, and the scores never surprise me very much. The students I expect will get high or low scores usually do.

So, what do I do to assess my students? I look at their work. I assess their writing by looking at their writing, I assess reading by listening to them read and asking questions, and I assess progress in math the same way. By looking through their math portfolios I am able to assess their progress.

The following two chapters talk about how I use portfolios as a way of assessing my students' progress.

6 Presentation

My students share their solutions daily as part of math workshop. Sharing, discussing, answering questions, and explaining thinking are crucial parts of math workshop. But what happens after that problem has been sitting in a portfolio for three weeks? The specific skill or concept in that problem hasn't gone away, since we continually work on it, but that particular explanation and solution have. In order to make sure my students rethink problems they have already solved, I ask them to do periodic presentations (Figure 6.1).

Figure 6.1

Having children present their thinking in a more formal manner than in sharing sessions serves several purposes:

1. Formal presentations force kids to rethink a problem and solution. They may find alternative ways to solve a problem they solved weeks ago.
2. Presenting a problem formally requires very exact and specific explanations from the children. They need to be prepared to answer questions from their audience, so they need to know their subject matter well.
3. By rethinking and re-solving a problem already solved, understanding is reinforced. And at the same time, these presentations help me to assess if the child has a clear understanding of the problem and concept he is presenting.

One type of presentation I call a portfolio presentation and another, a concept presentation.

Portfolio Presentation

Every piece of work my students do during math workshop ends up in their math portfolios. These files become very large. When it is time for the kids to do a portfolio presentation, I usually go through the problems we have done and give them a choice of four or five to present. The kids pull these four or five problems from their portfolios and choose which of those to create a presentation for.

The kids have a handful of ideas for the types of presentations to do. We usually share these ideas before they begin.

"For this presentation, can we do anything we want?" Caitlin asked during a session about an upcoming presentation.

"What are some ideas you have?" I asked the class.

"Plays, puppet shows," Melissa said.

"A poster kind," Kathryn offered.

"We could do a game show maybe?" Kyle said.

"Cool! I'll do that with you, Kyle," Dave responded.

"What are the requirements of a presentation?" I asked.

"To make sure the audience can see and hear what you are presenting," answered Megan.

"Can we use things like cubes and stuff?" Gerek asked.

"Yeah, you can use anything," Megan said.

"After you choose your problem to present, you can begin working on your presentation," I tell my students.

Besides allowing kids to rethink problems, presentations give them a chance to try again at a later point a problem that may have been difficult at the first attempt. For example, Anna chose to present the following problem (Figure 6.2):

> There are 36 dogs on a team of dogsleds and six people. Each person needs to take care of a group of dogs. To make it fair, each person will take care of the same number of dogs. So how many dogs will each person have to take care of? Explain how you solved it.

When Anna solved this problem the first time during math workshop, she used unifix cubes to help her. She needed some help getting started.

"Do you have a question, Anna?" I asked as she came over to me.

"Yeah," she said.

"OK, can you read me the problem?" She read the problem back to me and, through questioning, counted out 36 unifix cubes and split them into six groups.

Weeks later, for the presentation, she decided to present this problem. She knew that she could have used unifix cubes as she had done the first time, but she decided to do a poster instead (Figure 6.3). She made a poster by cutting six people out of construction paper and gluing them onto the posterboard. She then cut out 36 dogs. When it was her time to present, she set her poster on an easel and proceeded to tell us what she was doing.

"There are these six people. And there are 36 dogs, and each of these people needs to take care of the same number of dogs. So, what they do is, they go onc for you, one for you, and like this," she said, gluing each dog to the poster as she spoke. When she had finished, she took questions and comments from the audience.

Figure 6.2

Thar are 6 dogs in Ach grop

I yosd Cuobs you 6 and Put Thim in to grops

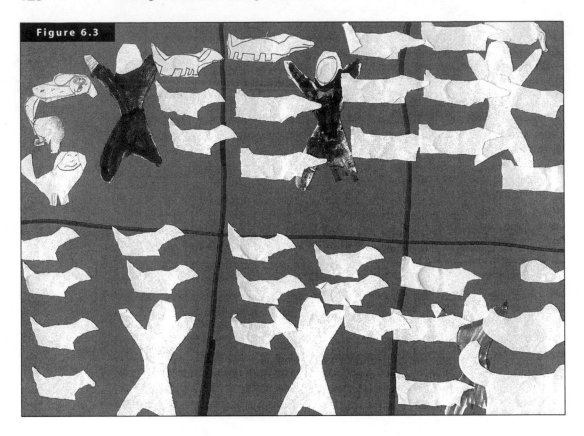

Figure 6.3

"That's a good poster, Anna, because I could see what you were doing," Megan said.

"I liked the way you actually cut out the dogs and put them up as we watched. It made it easy to understand what you were doing," Dave said.

"Did anyone not understand what Anna did?" I asked.

"How come some of the dogs have faces and look like dogs, and some just look like blobs?" Chris asked.

"Because I got tired of cutting out 36 dogs!" Anna laughed.

"Anna, I have a question," I said. "Why did you give each person six dogs and not some people four and others five? How come they all got six?"

"'Cause it said they all had to have the same number," she said, looking at me like I was nuts.

"Oh, so can you think of a name for what you did to the 36 to get 6?"

"Um, I did one for you, one for you; you mean like that? Like I divided it up?" she said.

"Yes, like that, Anna," I said, smiling. By having the opportunity to redo the problem, Anna was much more confident with her solution. When I questioned her the first time, when she solved the problem with unifix cubes, she was very unsure of her answer. Now, after she had more experience with division and problem solving, she was able to solve it on her own confidently.

During one portfolio presentation during our 1940s study, the kids were able to choose from all the problems they had worked on throughout the study. They could work alone, as partners, or in groups. If they chose to work in pairs or groups, the only requirement was that they share and discuss the problems before beginning their presentation. This requirement arose because of a difficulty during an earlier presentation. A group of kids working together couldn't agree on how to explain the solution. Each of them had solved the problem a different way. They decided to split up and not work together. We talked about what they could have done instead of splitting up. One of the kids thought they could have had a mock election. Each would present their explanation and solution, and they would let the audience vote on which child's they agreed with. An interesting idea; no one has ever tried it, so I don't know if it works.

These presentations ranged from drama to lecture-type talks. Kyle, Megan, Chris, and Ross presented the following problem as a game show:

■ Stamp Problem

A stamp in 1942 cost 3 cents. A stamp today costs 32 cents.

What is the difference in price between 1942 and 1996?

How much money would it have cost to mail six letters in 1942?

How much money would it cost to mail six letters today?

Explain your solutions.

Kyle was the game show host. Megan, Chris, and Ross dressed up as contestants in the game show. Kyle asked the questions, and they answered them and explained how they got their answers. For instance, Kyle directed a question to Ross by speaking into a microphone made out of a funnel and white paper, in his best game-show-host voice, "OK, Mr. Ross, a stamp in 1942 cost 3 cents and today a stamp costs 32 cents. So, can you tell me the difference in price between 1942 and 1996?"

"Why, yes, I can," Ross answered. "That would be 29 cents."

"And, Mr. Ross, just how did you come up with 29 cents?" the host asked Ross.

"I just took 3 away from 32 and that would be 29. See? I start at 32 and count backwards three times. 31, 30, 29."

"Very nicely done Mr. Ross." Kyle said. He went on to ask questions of the other contestants.

Besides the presentations serving as a way for the kids to rethink their own solutions, they are a time for those listening to hear a different twist on a problem they have already solved. Many times a student will understand something better after watching the presentations. I remember when a student presented her graph paper bridge and was explaining how she calculated the volume of her bridge supports.

"The supports of my bridge were made with 1 inch graph paper, see? So when I needed to figure out the volume, I just decided to use those wooden cubes, since they are also 1 inch. Or about 1 inch, I think. I filled up the support with cubes and got 9. You say 9 cubic inches and it's easy to remember because, see, the cubes are cubes."

"Oh, now I get it. It's just filling up," shouted Anna. She hadn't understood volume at the time we were constructing bridges. But at this presentation, which happened a few months later, she was able to watch, listen, and better understand the concept. Not that she internalized the idea of volume after that presentation—she didn't need to—but she was able to understand that volume meant "filling up." Sometimes, it just takes a child's explanation to get a point across. Presentations do this beautifully.

Concept Presentation

The other type of presentation I ask my students to create is based on specific concepts. For instance, I might ask them to create a presentation on fractions. That is all I would say. It becomes their job to find a pertinent problem to share. That way, I not only get the opportunity to see what my kids know about fractions but I also am able to see what they know about writing fraction problems and how they present what they know to an audience.

I gave my fourth, fifth, and sixth graders the following presentation assignment:

> You are going to do another math presentation, although this one is slightly different. You will choose which concept to present. After you choose your concept, you will need to follow certain guidelines in your presentation.
>
> Choose one of the following concepts to do your presentation on:
>
> - Fractions
> - Circumference
> - Division
> - A different base system, like 5 or 4
> - Multiplication
>
> After you choose your concept, follow these guidelines to do your presentation:
>
> 1. Write a problem that is challenging but not so challenging that you can't solve it. If you can solve it without much work, rethink how challenging it was for you. (This problem should be a word-type problem, not just 23 × 12.)
> 2. Figure out a way to present this problem. It will need to be large enough so that an audience can see it, hear you, and understand what you are presenting. You can do anything you want as long as you can answer questions correctly about your presentation.

3. When you practice your presentation, assume that no one in your audience will understand anything you are about to do. Speak clearly, and explain every step you are presenting. Your presentation should clearly show you understand what you are doing.

4. Be prepared. If you have handouts, make sure you have them all ready. You should practice your presentation a few times before doing it.

When you have practiced and are ready, write up an explanation about what your presentation will show your audience. In your explanation, you should include why you chose the concept you did, what your presentation will teach your audience, and how you will know if your audience understood what you were presenting. Turn this explanation in to me just before your presentation.

One of the requirements was to practice their presentations and to be prepared. The kids practiced their presentations for their parents during portfolio conference. This practice gave them a good idea as to whether they were prepared, if their presentation made sense, if it was challenging enough, and if they fully understood the concept they were presenting. After the conference practice, the kids had a chance to revise their presentations before they did them for the class.

The presentations varied greatly. Chris did a presentation on circumference. He wrote the following problem for us to solve:

If Lou and Brad cut down a tree that was 8 inches in radius and 16 inches in diameter, what is the circumference?

Explain.

Chris wrote his problem on the whiteboard and had a paper tree that he had made with the dimensions of the tree in his problem. After the audience had come up with solutions and shared them, Chris explained how he had solved his own problem and described circumference.

"Well, first, I measured it the easy way. I just took this string and wrapped it around the trunk of the tree. Then I measured the string using a ruler. Then I did it the other way, the way we figured out in class. We figured out in class that pi was 3.14. Remember when we did that thing where most of our answers were around 3, and we decided that pi was around 3? And when we looked up pi, it was 3.14? Well, I used 3.14 and times-ed it by the diameter, which was 16. The formula for circumference is pi times diameter. I didn't tell you to find the area, but that's pi times the radius squared."

Chris could answer questions about his presentation. He knew that circumference wasn't just a formula, since he knew that he could also wrap a string around the tree to find the solution. He knew that circumference was really the number you get when you "wrap around" something. From his presentation, I learned more about what Chris knew on this concept than I would have if I'd simply asked him to solve circumference equations on a worksheet.

The presentation explanations the kids were asked to write were interesting. Cory wrote about her presentation on base 7:

> I am doing base 7 problems because I like to do different bases and I think base 7 will help you learn the 7's times table too. It will teach the audience how to convert base 10 into base 7. I will know the audience understands if they can figure out the weight of the spaceship in base 7 because that one is really challenging. It will show the audience an interesting way to learn about base 7.

Megan wrote about her fraction presentation:

> My presentation will show the audience how to do fractions. I chose to do fractions because I have been doing fractions since first grade and I am familiar with them. How I'll know people know what I'm talking about is I'll ask them.

Kim wrote about her presentation on division with a different base system:

> My presentation will show the class how to divide in a base. I chose this concept because it's something new. We (the class) haven't done division in bases yet. The way I will know if the class understood is by my handouts.

These presentations showed me what my students knew about the concepts they chose to share. Kim knew a lot about different base systems and division. I already knew this, but I didn't know what she knew about dividing in different base systems. I learned much from her presentation, not only about division but also about how she approached her solutions and how she had figured this out on her own.

She began by showing us a poster she had made showing the base 6 pieces (Figure 6.4). The mat was a 6×6 array, the strip was a 6×1 array, and the unit was a 1×1 array. She wrote $422_6 \div 3_6$ and then explained how she went about dividing in base 6.

"First, I made four mats, two strips, and two units and glued them down. Then I figured out what 422_6 was in base 10. That was 124_{10}. I got 124_{10} by multiplying 36_{10} by 4_{10}, since I had four mats of 36_{10}. That was 144_{10}. Then, the two strips of 6_{10}, which is 12_{10}, so 144_{10} plus 12_{10} is 156_{10}, and the two units are just 2_{10}, so the total is 158_{10}. So $422_6 = 158_{10}$. The next thing I did was to divide 158_{10} by 3_{10}. Then I got 52.6_{10}. All I did next was to change that back into base 6. I got one mat, two strips, and four units. So $422_6 \div 3_6 = 124_6$."

Sound confusing? It was for me! The class seemed to understand her explanation easily, but it took me a while and I asked a lot of questions. I think what struck me was how she changed the base 6 number into base 10 before dividing it. Since she did this on her own, without ever doing much division with other base systems, I thought her solution was interesting and

Figure 6.4

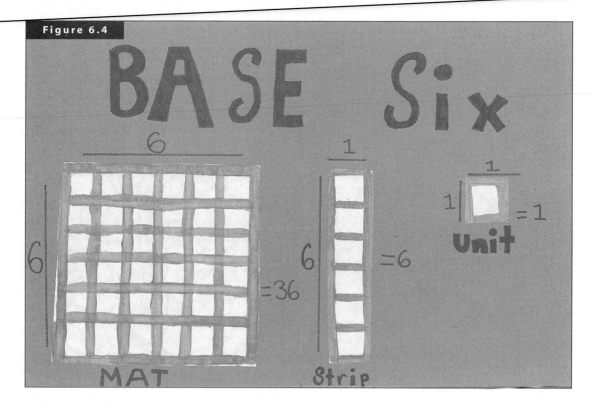

very telling of how she was looking at different bases. Generally, as Aisha explained to me, we like kids to think in the base system they are in, and we discourage changing back into base 10. Kim was quick at this conversion, and it showed me that she understood the relation between the two. But from her presentation I feared that she had showed the other kids a "trick" that I didn't want them using. I wanted the kids to think about division of base systems using the pieces in that base system. So here was a dilemma. Her presentation was finished, she had explained how she got her solution, she clearly knew how to manipulate and calculate different base systems, and she was confident in her explanation. Should I tell her it was not the right way? I decided to question her instead.

"Kim, that's great, but I have some questions I'd like you to consider. The rest of you can too," I began. "We have been doing a lot of work with different base systems, and we haven't been changing from base 10 and back again. Can you think of another way to do the division without doing that?"

"Well, yeah. I guess the easiest way would be to use the pieces. Like, get out four mats, two strips, and two units and split them up into three groups," she said matter-of-factly.

"That sounds easier to do when learning about it, don't you think? Can you show us how you would do this?" I asked. And she had us all make the pieces and put them into three groups.

This taught me that I needn't worry so much about questioning my students. Through this presentation Kim taught me that she was ready to do some more challenging problems, and she showed the class how dividing in different base systems wasn't all that different from dividing in base 10. Had I told her not to do this presentation because we hadn't talked about it yet, it would have been a poor decision on my part. Her presentation turned out to be really more of a lesson than a presentation of what she already knew.

These presentations teach me much more about my students than a test does. I learn what my kids know about problems they have already solved or about particular concepts, how they will approach a presentation, why they have chosen to present what they do, how they will explain their thinking to an audience, and just how confident they are with what they are talking about. Presentations are one type of formal assessment my students take part in during the year.

7

Assessment, Conferences, Reporting

The assessments I care about and share with parents is the progress my students are making over time, what they know, and how they know it. Parents view their children's work during conferences led by the child. I make it a point to educate the parents on authentic assessments we do in class. Then they too begin to know what to look for and how to take standardized tests with a grain of salt.

The problem today is the pressure school districts are putting on teachers about test scores. In Oregon, for example, the scores for each school district are published in the newspaper. In the local papers the district scores are then broken down by school. The implication is that schools with higher test scores are better than those with lower scores. It's awful! What do these tests tell us about students? Because of a number of complex problems, many of which are beyond the control of the individual teacher, some schools will *always* score lower than others. Prior experience is so crucial to children as they enter school. Just because some schools score lower on standardized tests doesn't mean the students there aren't learning or aren't challenged. The best schools are those in which the teachers and students work hard and concentrate on progress and growth, where teachers respect and are connected to their children, and where teachers hold high expectations for all of their students.

Assessment

How do I assess my students? I look at their work. I know what they can do by observing how they solve problems, watching and listening to how they share solutions, reading what they write about their thinking, and seeing how they answer questions I or other children ask them. Assessment means learning about my students. Learning how they learn, what strategies they use to learn, and when they make progress is the way I assess my students' learning. The best way I can learn about my students and observe their progress is to look closely at their work.

I also use assessment as a tool to improve my teaching. If I don't observe my students and record their progress, how can I grow and adjust my teaching practice? When I observed that my kids' spelling on drafts wasn't improving with weekly spelling tests, I stopped giving those tests. I found better ways for them to learn spelling than just memorization. When I began looking at how my students could create their own algorithms, I knew I needed to step back and not teach them the way I had been taught. Through authentic assessments and by looking at my students' work, I believe my teaching has become better over the years.

When I need to write up a report or get ready for conferences, I look through my students' work. Just giving a test and grading it would tell me nothing about how the child was thinking. Math tests don't work for me. If I want to know whether my students know how to add numbers, I'll ask them to show me—sometimes in the form of a presentation, at other times just on a piece of paper. For instance, I often give my students a choice of several raw equations and have them write about how they solved them. Eight-year-old Laura was given a choice of the following equations:

$18 - 5$ $26 - 13$ $45 - 36$ $90 - 13$ $246 - 179$

I asked her to choose one of these to solve and then write about how she solved it. She chose to solve $246 - 179$ and wrote the following:

1. I used cubes to take 9 away from 16 but first I had to borrow 10 from the 10's group. And $16 - 9 = 7$.
2. Then I moved onto the next two numbers, which were 4 and 7. But since I had to borrow on the last two numbers, the 4 had become a 3. You can't take 7 away from 3, though! So I had to borrow from the next 10's group. So then the numbers became 13 and 7, so once again I used the cubes to take 7 away from 13. In the end, $13 - 7 = 6$.
3. Now, here it comes, the easy part! $2 - 1$. But, remember, I had to borrow! So it is $1 - 1$ and that is tremendously easy! It is 0! So my final answer for the whole problem . . . the answer is 67.

From this explanation I learned that Laura knew the meaning of *borrow* in terms of subtraction. I learned that she uses cubes to help her subtract and that she knows about place value, since she knew, for example, that the 6 became a 16. And I learned that she can write about mathematics in a strong voice. This is much more useful to me when getting a picture of a student than a simple page of subtraction problems would have been. This sheet went into her portfolio, and she could use it during a conference to explain to her parents what she knew about subtraction.

I am often asked what I do with the "slower" kids, the ones who can't meet the state or district benchmarks or goals. I'm not sure how to answer that question. What should I do? At the beginning of the year I assess where each student is in terms of mathematical development. I teach from there. All children learn at different rates and make progress at different times. Some of my students make more progress than others, even though they don't reach the benchmarks. For example, Cody, a first grader, came into class barely knowing how to count to 10. He couldn't write numbers and wasn't too sure what a number was. Jake, on the other hand, also a first grader, could add high numbers, write numbers with many digits, and think mathematically in a concrete way. How on earth could I assess these two children in the same way? Cody wasn't slow or low; he was just Cody. I never use words like *low* or *high* when referring to my students; I just can't. They are who they are.

Cody ended the year being able to add numbers and solve a variety of problems with confidence. He made more progress that year than any child I had ever seen, even though he couldn't do all that the state said he should be able to do at his grade level. It's important to remain focused on how a child progresses and whether he makes progress. Had Cody made *no* progress in math, I would have been concerned. I would also have been concerned if Jake had made no progress during the year, even though he far surpassed what the state said he should be able to do. States, districts, and schools need to look at children as individuals, not as groups of children all at the same place. Just because a group of second graders are all eight years old doesn't mean they are all the same type of learners and at the same place in their development.

All of the sharing the kids do during math sharing time is one of the most powerful assessments I have. Listening to what they know and how they explain their thinking is something you just can't get on a test. When Cody explained a problem for the first time all year, and with total confidence in his solution and thinking strategy, he had made progress not only with the concept he was explaining but also with his confidence in himself as a mathematician and in his ability to explain his thinking. What better assessment is there than the real and authentic work that students do?

These mental notes and observations help me to write reports and prepare for conferences. I use these mental notes along with the kids' portfolios as the foundation for assessing my students.

Math Portfolios

Everything goes in the kids' math portfolios. Everything. By June these files are thick and packed full of a year's worth of work. Every assignment, problem, note, and anything else that is related to math in any way is filed in these portfolios. Some teachers can send things home after reports are written or grades are given out, others only save a few pieces of work. For portfolios to work for me, I feel more comfortable saving it all. At the end of the year, I send home the entire file. I use a plastic file box with hanging files. Actually, these files aren't as huge as one might think. I suppose if I were to use workbooks there would be hundreds of pages of ripped-out sheets. But since I don't, these files are fat but manageable.

In preparation for a portfolio conference or for a report, I ask the kids to go through their math files and choose specific pieces of work to share with their parents.

Conferences

We do student-led conferences in my class. The children prepare, practice, and present their work to their parents. I am there to answer questions and offer some other comments when the child is finished.

In preparing for the conference, the kids are given a conference folder. For the first conference in September, which is a goal-setting conference, I give the kids a few things to think about. They write about the following:

This year I want to challenge myself by _____.
This year I want to show my independence by _____.
This year I will show that I respect members of my community by

_____.

The kids complete these sentences, and then this sheet gets stapled to the left side of their conference folder. (This is a manila file folder that stays with me until the child leaves my room. Some kids will have the same conference folder for three years.)

On the right side of the folder there is a sheet explaining the work samples the kids have chosen to share. These change from conference to conference. For instance, for one conference I asked the kids to collect the following samples for their folders:

- Pieces of writing showing description, editing, and progress
- Research
- A favorite book
- Math samples: a problem; addition/subtraction/multiplication/division
- Art
- A project

As the kids chose these samples, they checked them off.

It is difficult to put a project or a large piece of artwork into the folder, so the rule is, if it doesn't fit or it's no longer at school, they have to write about it and draw a picture of what it looked like. Kyle, for example, wrote about a photograph I had taken of one of his 1940s math presentations. The photo was glued to a piece of paper, and he wrote the following below it:

Me, Chris, Ross, and Megan did a game show of the stamp problem. And there were three questions. But first you needed to know that a stamp in 1942 cost 3 cents. Well, these are the questions. I asked Ross this question, What is the difference in price between 1942 and 1996? My answer was 29, Ross said out loud. And how did you do it? I asked him. He said that he just took away 3 cents from 32 cents. And the second one I did was to ask how much money would it cost to mail six letters in 1942? And Megan said that her answer was 18 cents. How she did it was say that she just did 3 cents six times. And the last question was how much money would it cost to mail six letters in 1996? And how Chris did it was he said his answer was whatever 32 cents times 3 was. Then I doubled that, and my answer was $1.92.

For one February conference, which in my district was the last formal conference of the year, the kids completed the following statements:

I am a writer because _____.
I am a mathematician because _____.
I am a reader because _____.
I am an important member of this community because _____.

They also wrote about the progress they had made in specific areas. They completed the following statements:

I have improved as a reader by _____.
To continue improving as a reader, I need to _____.
I have become a better writer by _____.
To continue improving as a writer, I need to _____.
I have improved as a mathematician by _____.
To continue improving as a mathematician, I need to _____.
I have improved as an independent and community member of this
    class by _____.
To continue improving as an independent and community member of
    this class, I need to _____.

The kids don't do all this writing in one sitting. Usually, I have them write on a couple of questions each day leading up to the conference. Some of the older kids, the ones who are used to doing this, will complete it in one sweep, but I make sure the others have as much time as they need. I don't want to rush them, because they know it is important and that their parents will be reading it. So we usually begin getting ready a week before.

Sometimes, we have specific focuses for a portfolio conference. I like to hold portfolio nights where the parents can come and view their children's work. These are a bit more informal than a conference in that the parents are not given a 30 minute time slot as they are during conference days. Instead, all the parents and children come during a span of an hour and a half at night. One such portfolio night we focused on research.

The year we had become Kidsville the kids researched different aspects of our town. Kyle researched lawyers, since he was a member of the law-makers in our community. He wrote about his research and shared his draft and final copy with his parents.

That same portfolio night we also shared the number studies they were working on.

The day before a conference or the day of a portfolio night, the kids practice presenting their portfolios. They choose partners and trade off being the student and the parent. The partner who is the parent listens and asks questions about what she is hearing. This allows the child to practice sharing his portfolio. I tell the kids that if they don't talk during their conference, it will be very quiet! This practice really helps. All the kids are ready and prepared during the actual conference.

I write letters to the parents explaining to them how to listen to their child during a conference. I do this so that the child is not intimidated or nervous that his parents will quiz him. Once a father totally humiliated his daughter during a conference by deliberately quizzing her on things she didn't know, so I decided that maybe a letter explaining questioning techniques would be helpful.

Following is a portion of the letter I wrote for a portfolio conference for the parents of my fourth, fifth, and sixth graders:

> This is a portfolio conference. In a conference such as this, there are some guidelines that the children and I would like you to be aware of. This is a time to listen to your child explain their work to you. This is not a time to quiz your child about their work.
>
> For instance, you may see things throughout the portfolio that you may view as a mistake or wrong. Remember that this is a working folder of your child's work in school. They are here to explain aspects of their learning strategies to you. They are not here to show you just their work that is neat and correct. They want to share their real work that they partake in on a daily basis. And that work is messy, hard, involved, and full of strategies for figuring out new information.
>
> Please do not throw out testing questions to your child or ask why an answer is wrong. Please just listen to your child and try to understand what process they have gone through to find a solution to whatever piece of work they are sharing with you.
>
> Some of you have never been to a student-led conference before, and these guidelines may be helpful to you.
>
> Thank you from all of us—we hope you learn a lot from what we have been learning!

When the parents are finished listening to their child, they are free to write comments to me about how the conference went.

I keep the conference portfolios until the child has left my class. It is wonderful for parents to see the progress their child has made over the years by looking through the folder.

Reports

The other type of formal assessment I do is reporting to parents. I don't grade my students using traditional grading systems. I have been fortunate in the schools where I've worked in that I am not required to give a letter or number grade to my students. Instead, I choose to write narrative reports on progress, learning styles, and learning strategies. How could I give a child one grade for math? If I had to give a child a B in math, for instance, would that mean the child has a B in computation *and* fractions *and* patterning *and* geometry? What does a grade mean? A grade doesn't tell a parent how and why a child can do what she does. I believe it is up to me to write to parents about their children as learners.

This year I had a number of parents call me after their first middle school conference. Several of them told me that when they were told their child's grade for the term, they said to the teacher, "I don't care about the grade. Tell me what my child can do." I was happy to hear that response. It reinforced my belief that if parents are educated about authentic assessments and taught to look at what their children can do, they will be less inclined to focus just on a grade. If you are required to give a letter grade, as most teachers are, I suggest you write a short narrative to go along with the report card. The example narratives that follow are quite lengthy, and yours certainly don't have to be this detailed.

I have written many different types of narrative reports over the years. Sometimes they are very long narratives and sometimes they are shorter pieces focusing on a specific piece of work.

Here is a portion of a report I wrote on Carly as a mathematician. This section focuses on number sense:

> Carly is able to solve mathematical problems using a variety of strategies and by creating her own methods for solutions. She can use the concepts of addition, subtraction, multiplication, division, fractions, area, estimation, measurement, time, place value, and different base systems. She is an incredible problem solver. She will explain her solutions using complex charts and/or graphs, pictures, and writing. Her explanations are always extremely complete and well thought out. She is always going beyond what is expected of her during math workshop, as she is constantly challenging herself.
>
> She is able to challenge herself with specific problems I write as well as with open-ended problems I pose. With one such open-ended

problem, she was asked to explain the number 875. She came up with five ways to do this. One, she drew 8 hundreds squares, 7 tens strips, and 5 square units and then wrote an explanation underneath that said, "This means 800, this means 70, and this means five 1's." She wrote an equation: 800 + 70 + 5. She also wrote that 875 is an odd number, and that $8.75 is one $5 bill, four $1 bills, and three quarters.

All of this tells me several things about Carly as a mathematician. Number one, she is able to use language to explain her thinking strategies. Number two, she has a solid sense of place value, and number three, she is able to challenge herself to go as far as she can with a problem, no matter how challenging or simple the problem may be.

She has shown what numbers look like in different base systems. For example, she was asked to show what the number 27 looked like in base 10 and base 5. She drew 27 as 2 ten strips and 7 units in base 10; and as 5 fives strips and 2 units in base 5. She then challenged herself to try it in base 3 and drew 9 threes strips. Working in different base systems will ultimately strengthen her multiplication skills.

Carly will help others during problem-solving groups or partnerships. She is aware of the math levels of all the children and will adjust her explanations for those she is talking to. (A natural teacher!)

She contributes at Calendar and is learning to not shout out answers but to give others "thinking time" to try and figure out what she can do quickly. She is a wonderful leader at Calendar and asks specific questions.

This narrative told her parents much more about Carly as a mathematician than a single grade would have done.

The following year I focused my narrative on samples of work. Here is the written portion of Kyle's report. It's a little hard to follow because the actual four pieces of work were attached to his original report, but it should give you an idea of how it worked.

I have chosen four problems to reflect on. The first was a simple problem that basically asked what 9 × 5 was. The reason I chose it was to show Kyle's unique thinking strategy. He solved this problem in two ways, since it was not very challenging for him. The first way he solved it was to count by tens. I love the way he described this: "All I did was count by tens and whenever I did a ten I'd lift up two fingers." He also counted by fives.

The second problem was extremely challenging and Kyle stuck with it. It asked a very challenging question and Kyle solved it by organizing the steps. He then added in his head until he got a solution. The final number was very large, and he did a great job setting this problem up (*the* most important step for problem solving).

The third problem I chose because it was another simple problem for him to solve, but he discovered five different ways to solve it. I think the drawing of "what went on in my head" is wonderful!

The last problem I chose was a small problem I gave him to solve and explain his thinking. His explanation clearly demonstrates his ability to create a multistep algorithm. He writes how he solved 624 + 389: "I just put the 89 and the 24 aside and added 600 to 300 and that was 900. And then I added 24 and then I put the 9 from the 89 aside and added 80 to 924 and that was 1004 and then I added the 9." What knowledge this child has for place value! He understands addition of high numbers so well that he could use any algorithm that is presented to him. I only hope he is never stifled to solve problems just one way. He is much too intelligent and creative for that!

He solves any problem I give him. Nothing is too challenging for him. He can solve computation equations for addition, subtraction, multiplication, division, or fractions. He is able to organize and set up any type of problem and attempt to come up with a solution. What a mathematician this child is!

Kyle is able to share, explain, and present his problems to the entire class. He explains his thinking very clearly so that even some of the younger children understand how he came up with his solutions. He is a great teacher as well—he often helps some of the children in the class who need his assistance.

When the work samples were sent home, the parents were able to see what I was writing about. The kids also wrote reflections on their own work. They reflected on their work informally throughout the year and formally for a written report, their portfolio, or for a parent conference.

It is time-consuming to write narrative reports, but I believe it is time well spent. Brenda Power's books *Taking Note* and *Well-Chosen Words* give information on note-taking strategies and advice on writing narrative reports and comments on report cards.

All professionals write notes about their clients or patients. Doctors take notes, lawyers take notes . . . teachers can write notes about their students. I don't think everyone should write narratives as extensive as mine, but some form of note or comment about learning strategies and styles is important information for parents and teachers.

The Last Word

It is the practice of teaching, the growing sense of self as a teacher, and the continual inquisitiveness about new and better ways to teach and learn that serve teachers in their quest to understand and change the practice of teaching.

—*NCTM Curriculum Standards*

Children are mathematical geniuses. There is so much more knowledge in their heads than we give them credit for. Young children can learn so much more than we teach them; we just need to let them show us. Let's stop rushing them through an impractical continuum of requirements. We can trust children to learn at their own pace without labeling them "low" or "high."

There is more to becoming a writer than learning letters, sounds, and punctuation; there is more to becoming a mathematician than learning facts, algorithms, and methods. The heart of learning is not in the pieces but in the richness of the understanding and the joy of discovery. One is the shell, the other, the core. When the core is reached, nurtured, and energized, the shell settles more easily into place.

My hope is that we will nurture the core in all young mathematicians, all young learners.

Appendix: Problems and NCTM Standards

Here are the thirteen NCTM Standards for K–4:

1. Mathematics as Problem Solving
2. Mathematics as Communication
3. Mathematics as Reasoning
4. Mathematical Connections
5. Estimation
6. Number Sense and Numeration
7. Concepts of Whole Number Operations
8. Whole Number Computation
9. Geometry and Spatial Sense
10. Measurement
11. Statistics and Probability
12. Fractions and Decimals
13. Patterns and Relationships

There are also NCTM Standards for grades 5–8, and there are many consistencies within these two groups of standards. In fact, the first four standards are identical. The rest of the standards for grades 5–8 are as follows: number and number relationships; number systems and number theory; computation and estimation; patterns and functions; algebra; statistics; probability; geometry; and measurement. During the year I taught my fourth, fifth, and sixth graders I referred to both sets of standards.

Several standards are incorporated in each of the problems I write for my students and most problems include the first four, which are common to both sets of standards. Throughout the book I have indicated which K–4 standards are included in the problems. The children solve the problems, write and share their solutions and strategies, think about their organization and if their solutions make sense, and make mathematical connections

Problem Title	Text Page	K–4 Standards Numbers
M&M Problem	28	1, 2, 3, 4, 6, 7, 8
Arctic Store Problem	36	1, 2, 3, 4, 5, 6, 8
Arctic People Problem	37	1, 2, 3, 4, 6, 7, 8
Walnut Problem	38	1, 2, 3, 4, 5, 6, 7, 8, 11, 12
Trip to Ellis Island	39	1, 2, 3, 4, 5, 6, 7, 8, 9, 12
Time Travel Machine	40	1, 2, 3, 4, 6, 9, 12
Victory Garden Problem	40	1, 2, 3, 4, 6, 9, 12
Creating Circumference	46	1, 2, 3, 4, 5, 9, 10
Design Book	50	1, 2, 3, 4, 6, 9, 10, 12, 13
Factory Problem	80	1, 2, 3, 4, 6, 7, 8, 12
Victory Garden: 2	80	1, 2, 3, 4, 6, 10
Schools of the Future	96	1, 2, 3, 4, 5, 6, 7, 8, 9, 10, 12, 13
Hide a Family	99	1, 2, 3, 4, 5, 6, 7, 8, 9, 10, 12, 13
Design a House	102	1, 2, 3, 4, 5, 6, 7, 8, 9, 10, 11, 12

between the problems they solve. With open-ended problems, different standards are incorporated, depending on what the children choose to do with the problem. I include estimation (Standard 5) in most of the problems the children begin. I ask them to estimate what they think the solution might be and how they came up with that estimate.

In addition to the problems that appear in the text, I have included here some problems that I've written over the years. I've chosen fairly randomly to give you an idea of the variety of problems I write. For each problem, I show the K–4 NCTM Standards it incorporates.

■ A1

You want to share 43 cookies with 25 friends.

How many cookies do you *think* each friend will get?

How many cookies *will* each friend get?

Explain your thinking.

NCTM Standards: 1, 2, 3, 4, 5, 6, 7, 8

■ A2

What is the area and perimeter of a 6 × 9 array using the medium-sized graph paper?

Show your work.

NCTM Standards: 1, 2, 3, 4, 10

■ A3

Draw a right angle (a 90° angle).

Draw an angle that is half as open as the 90° angle. How many degrees is that angle?

Draw an angle that is twice as open as the 90° angle. How many degrees is that angle?

Explain.

NCTM Standards: 1, 2, 3, 4, 9

■ A4

Show a town with an area of 12 square units.

Color 1/2 of the town brown.

Color 1/2 blue.

How did you do it?

NCTM Standards: 1, 2, 3, 4, 6, 10, 12

■ A5

Make a town with an area of 12 square units.

Color 1/6 brown.

Color 1/6 blue.

Color 2/6 green.

Color 1/3 red.

How did you do it?

NCTM Standards: 1, 2, 3, 4, 6, 10, 12

■ **A6**

Make base _____ pieces.

Make units.

Make strips.

Make mats.

Make a strip-mat.

Make base _____ pieces.

Make units.

Make strips.

Make mats.

Make a strip-mat.

NCTM Standards: 1, 2, 3, 4, 6

■ **A7**

Do as many steps as you can on this problem:

1. Sam and Lisa each bought 16 sports cards.
2. One-fourth (1/4) of Sam's and Lisa's cards were football cards. One-fourth (1/4) were basketball cards. And 2/4 were baseball cards.
3. Sam traded 1/2 of his football cards and three of his baseball cards. Lisa traded 1/4 of her basketball cards and five baseball cards.
4. Sam and Lisa put their remaining cards together. They decided to separate them by type in a box. They had football, basketball, and baseball cards in the box.
5. They looked in the book and discovered that their football cards were worth $4.75, their basketball cards were worth $3.05, and their baseball cards were worth $12.35.
6. They read that if they kept their baseball cards for 10 years the value of the cards would double. They figured out how much they would be worth in 20 years and in 30 years.
7. Now, they did get money for the cards they traded. Sam got $9.25. He used that money to get more cards, but he only wanted to spend 1/3 of that money.
8. He wanted to buy packs of cards. Each pack held seven new cards, and each pack cost $1.75.
9. The change, and the rest of the money from the $9.25, he put in the bank. He already had $47.96 in his account.

10. At his bank, for a savings account he gets 10 percent in interest every month. He kept his money in the bank for six months.

Now go back to step 7 and write problems about what Lisa did with her money.

NCTM Standards: 1, 2, 3, 4, 6, 7, 8, 11, 12

■ A8

Make a bridge using the medium-sized graph paper. You may make the bridge stay together any way you want.

Here are your requirements:

1. The bridge needs three supports. Each support must be a 4×9 unit rectangle.
2. The bridge part that will go across the supports needs to be an 8×18 unit rectangle.

Tape the bridge together with the three supports underneath the bridge part.

Consider these questions:

1. What is the area of one support?
2. What is the area of all the supports together?
3. What is the area of the entire bridge?
4. What is the volume of one support?
5. What is the volume of all the supports together?
6. What is the volume of the entire bridge?
7. What is volume? How is it different from area?

NCTM Standards: 1, 2, 3, 4, 5, 10

■ A9

At the Kids' Café, we made $11 the first week, $12 the second week, and $13 the third week. How much money did we make altogether?

If we make about the same amount every week, how much can we expect to make each month? in three months? in June?

If we split what we have made already in half, how much would we have? What about if we split it into thirds? into fourths?

If we need $50 to open a bank account, how much more money do we need?

If we make $10 next week, and $16 the following week, and $14 the week after that, what is the average amount of money we have made?

Take the total amount of money we have made so far. Double that number. Triple that number. Quadruple that number.

Let's say we make three times the total we have now, and then spend $23. Then we make back about 1/3 of what we spent. How much money would we have then?

Make a bar graph, a circle graph, and a line graph on separate pieces of paper that will show how much money we are making at our café.

NCTM Standards: 1, 2, 3, 4, 6, 7, 8, 12

■ A10

During Kwanza, seven candles are lit each night. During Chanukah, nine candles are lit on the last night (eight plus one shamash).

If there were five families celebrating Kwanza and four families celebrating Chanukah, how many candles would be lit on the last night of each festival?

Explain your solution.

NCTM Standards: 1, 2, 3, 4, 6, 8

■ A11

You are going to can some food. You have 25 jars. It will take you 15 minutes to can three jars of food.

How long will it take you to finish all 25 jars?

How did you solve this problem?

NCTM Standards: 1, 2, 3, 4, 6, 8

■ A12

You have a full glass of milk, but you spill 1/4 of the milk. Then you spill 1/2 of what was left!

How much milk do you have left now?

Show your work in pictures.

Written by Chris/Ashley/Alicia

NCTM Standards: 1, 2, 3, 4, 12

■ A13

You are inviting eight friends to a party. Each friend will need three party favors. Each party favor costs 35 cents.

How many party favors do you need to buy?

How much will it cost you?

Explain.

Written by Dave/Carly/Morgan

NCTM Standards: 1, 2, 3, 4, 6, 7, 8

■ **A14**

It was −25°F in Fairbanks. It was 43°F in Portland.

How much colder was it in Fairbanks?

Explain how you did this.

NCTM Standards: 1, 2, 3, 4, 5, 6, 8

■ **A15**

Fifty years from now, what year will it be?

How old will you be?

Explain how you got those answers.

You used your picture phone for one entire week six times a day. How many times did you use it that week?

If you used the phone only 1/2 as much, how many times would you have used it?

What if you used the phone twice as much? Then how often would you have used it?

Explain how you got your answers.

You decide to take a trip on a high-speed train. You can go 180 miles an hour.

You go somewhere that is three hours away. How many miles will you travel?

How long would it take to travel 450 miles?

If you could get a train that was twice as fast as that high-speed train, how many miles would the faster train travel in an hour?

Explain how you got your answers.

How old will you be in the year 2000?

How old will you be in the year 2036?

Explain.

NCTM Standards: 1, 2, 3, 4, 6, 7, 8, 12

■ **A16**

You have a backyard with an area of 1600 square feet. You want to plant a garden, build a deck, and put in a pool.

How many square feet will each of those be? Try to use as much space as you can.

Explain your solution.

NCTM Standards: 1, 2, 3, 4, 9, 10, 12

■ **A17**

Flour at the General Store costs 5 cents a pound. Potatoes cost 3 cents a pound. You need to buy four pounds of flour and three pounds of potatoes.

How much money did you spend?

How did you do it?

NCTM Standards: 1, 2, 3, 4, 8

■ **A18**

There are 24 houses and three people live in each house.

How many people are there all together?

How did you solve this?

There are four brothers and three sisters in a family. If no more than two children can share a room, and sisters and brothers do not sleep in the same room, how many bedrooms do the children use?

How did you solve this?

How many bedrooms will 16 kids need if they sleep no more than three to a room?

How did you solve this?

If 42 people live in six houses, how many people live in each house?

How did you solve this?

There are 24 people, and 1/4 of them live in apartments and 3/4 live in houses.

How many live in houses, and how many live in apartments?

How did you solve this?

There are 48 apartment houses, and 32 people live in each house.

How many people are there all together?

How did you solve this?

How many bedrooms will one house need if there are 35 people in the family and no more than three people can sleep in the same room?

How did you solve this?

How many houses will 160 people need if there can be no more than five people in each house?

How did you solve this?

There are 78 people, and 2/6 of them live in apartments and the rest live in houses.

How many live in apartments, and how many live in houses?

How did you solve this?

NCTM Standards: 1, 2, 3, 4, 6, 8, 12

■ **A19**

How long ago, how many years ago, was 1492?

How many years ago was the year 1279?

How many years ago was the year 56 B.C.E?

How did you get your answers?

According to the Hebrew calendar, it is the year 5757.

How many years older is the Hebrew calendar from our calendar?

Using the Hebrew calendar, what will the year be when our calendar says the year 2000?

How did you get your answers?

NCTM Standards: 1, 2, 3, 4, 5, 6, 7, 8

■ **A20**

It is 1996. We are traveling to 1943. How many years ago was that?

Explain how you got that solution.

NCTM Standards: 1, 2, 3, 4, 6, 8

■ **A21**

You want to make an island math game. Your game board must

Be the size of a piece of posterboard
Be the shape of our island
Be neatly drawn or painted
Have between 20 and 40 spaces
Have between five and eight "tricks"
Have a start space and a finish space
Have a name

Your cards will be

+ and − to and from 10
+ and − to and from 20
× and +

and can be

Straight flashcards
Word problems

Long equations
Whatever else you come up with

but they must all be of the same type.

Do things in this order:

1. Draft game board with no spaces.
2. Copy onto the posterboard in pencil.
3. Color or paint the game board.
4. Pencil in dots for the spaces.
5. Use stickers for the spaces.
6. Number the spaces, and write "start" and "finish."
7. Make the cards for the game.
8. Make between four and six pieces for the game.
9. Write rules for the game, and glue on back.
10. Name your game.
11. Put cards together with a rubber band, and place pieces and cards into a Zip-lock plastic bag.

NCTM Standards: 1, 2, 3, 4, 5, 6, 7, 8, 9

■ A22

Make an island with an area of 25 square units. Have the following things on or around the island:

- Eight palm trees. Make 1/2 of the trees with coconuts. Make 1/2 of the coconuts green.
- Six fish. Make 1/3 of the fish striped. Make 2/3 of the fish a solid color.
- Four people. Make 1/4 of the people in the water. Make 3/4 of the people on land. Put one of the land people up in a tree.
- Two boats. Make 1/2 of one boat brown. Make the other 1/2 black. Make the other boat have four sails. Have 1/4 of the sails higher than the rest.

Name your island.

NCTM Standards: 1, 2, 3, 4, 6, 7, 10, 12

■ A23

A team of travelers is having a problem. They have six kayaks that each hold two people. But there are 13 people on the team.

How many people will be able to travel in the kayaks?

Will there be any extra people?

What should they do?

Explain your answer.

NCTM Standards: 1, 2, 3, 4, 6, 8

■ **A24**

In a time machine, you go 16 years into the future. What year are you in?

Then you go backwards from that year 53 years. Now what year are you in?

OK, so now … how many years did you travel in all?

Written by Kyle/Jordan/Caitlin

NCTM Standards: 1, 2, 3, 4, 6, 7, 8

■ **A25**

You need to create a market. You can decide what the prices will be, but all prices will be by the pound. You need vegetables, fruit, meat, and baking goods.

Make a list of your goods and the prices at which you will sell them. Then exchange sheets with another group and go shopping at their market; they will shop at yours.

You get $25 to spend. Make a shopping list of what you want. Make a price list of what you spent. Compare your lists with each other.

NCTM Standards: 1, 2, 3, 4, 5, 6, 8

■ **A26**

How many things can you find in the room that are 8 inches long? What are they?

Written by Morgan/Alissa/Megan

NCTM Standards: 1, 2, 3, 4, 10

■ **A27**

You want to buy some candy, so you save your money and go to the store. You go to the store five times, and buy three pieces of candy each time you go. But, one time, you dropped and lost two pieces of candy.

So, how many pieces of candy do you have now altogether?

Explain.

Written by Paige/Shanti/Jacob

NCTM Standards: 1, 2, 3, 4, 6, 8

■ **A28**

You want to go to the park four times a day for five days. But one day you can only go twice, and another day you can only go three times. How many times will you be going to the park altogether?

Explain your thinking.

NCTM Standards: 1, 2, 3, 4, 5, 6, 7, 8

■ **A29**

You are putting together a party. You have $65 to spend. You buy a cake for $13, plates for $8, napkins for $4, and ice cream for $15.

How much money will you have left? What will you spend it on?

Explain.

NCTM Standards: 1, 2, 3, 4, 6, 7, 8

■ **A30**

On a hot summer day, the temperature was 100°F. A storm blew in and the temperature dropped 30 percent.

What was the temperature then?

Explain.

You want to buy a shirt that costs $50. You notice that there is a sale and you can take 10 percent off the price of the shirt.

How much do you pay for the shirt?

Explain.

You and a friend go out for lunch. The bill comes to exactly $14. You need to leave a 15 percent tip.

How much do you leave?

Explain.

You have a savings account that gives you 6 percent of your total savings every month. This month you have $125 in your account.

How much will you earn this month?

Explain.

NCTM Standards: 1, 2, 3, 4, 6, 12

■ **A31**

I went looking for foam board this weekend. Here's what I found:

Office Depot: pack of three pieces for $6.99
Michaels: one piece for $2.99

We need 54 pieces of foam board for our house-building project. I want to know which of the two stores will give us the better deal.

Why and how did you come to this conclusion?

How much will it cost to buy the amount we need?

If we go with the Office Depot three-pack, how many packs will we need? How much will that cost?

We also need X-acto knives for this project. I found some for $1.99 apiece. How much would it cost to buy 26?

I also bought two packs of large chart paper. Each pack cost $9.99. How much did the two of them cost together?

Now add up the cost for the foam board, the knives, and the chart paper, and write down what it will cost so far to begin the project.

NCTM Standards: 1, 2, 3, 4, 5, 7, 8

■ **A32**

You have invited people to a Thanksgiving Day party. You need to buy five pumpkin pies and one turkey. You have $50 to spend. One pie costs $6. The turkey costs $13.

How much money did you spend on the pies?

How much money did you spend altogether?

How much money do you have left?

Explain your solution.

Your guests come into your house. You have 26 guests and five tables.

How many guests will be at each table?

Where will you sit?

Explain your solution.

Your guests are waiting for their pumpkin pie. You go to the kitchen to cut the pie into equal pieces. There are 27 people and five pies.

How do you cut your pies?

If there are any extra pieces, they need to be equally divided up for all 27 people.

Explain your solution.

Your guests are leaving. It is 8:15 P.M. They arrived at 4:00 P.M. You rented your five tables for $4 an hour.

How much money do you owe the rental company?

Explain your solution.

You have so much to clean up! Each of the 27 people used two plates and one cup. (You all ate with your fingers, so there wasn't any silverware.)

How many things do you need to wash up?

Explain your solution.

You must be very tired from your Thanksgiving Day party! How will you relax?

NCTM Standards: 1, 2, 3, 4, 5, 7, 8

■ A33

A girl is building six ice sculptures during the ice festival in her town in Finland. Her brother is building eight ice sculptures. At the end of the day, they put away their tools and go home to warm up.

The next morning, they notice that three of their sculptures have melted. While rebuilding, they end up making five sculptures.

A friend comes over with her nine sculptures that she doesn't want. The girl and her brother love them and add them to their collection.

But while they were eating dinner, a reindeer came by and knocked over six of their sculptures. There is no time to rebuild because the festival contest is the next morning.

How many ice sculptures do the girl and her brother bring to the contest?

Explain your solution.

NCTM Standards: 1, 2, 3, 4, 6, 8

■ A34

You have baked cookies for your Winter Solstice party. You baked 26 moon cookies, 24 sun cookies, and 20 star cookies.

You have invited 12 of your friends to come to the party. You want each of them to have the same number of moon, sun, and star cookies.

How will you do that?

Explain.

NCTM Standards: 1, 2, 3, 4, 6, 7, 8

■ **A35**

In your Victory Garden you are growing carrots. You told everyone in your family that when the carrots were ready to eat, you would share the carrots with them.

You pull out the carrots and count 37 carrots. There are four members in your family.

How many carrots can each person have?

Will there be any extras?

Explain.

NCTM Standards: 1, 2, 3, 4, 6, 8

■ **A36**

You are having an end-of-the-war party. You are baking cookies. You can put 18 cookies on each cookie sheet. You use three cookie sheets.

How many cookies will you bake?

You need to take the total number of cookies and give 1/4 of them to a neighbor.

How many cookies did you give the neighbor?

Explain your answers.

NCTM Standards: 1, 2, 3, 4, 6, 7, 8, 12

■ **A37**

It is now 1995. If we go 131 years into the future, what do you think the year will be?

How did you come up with your estimate?

Now find a solution. How did you figure that out?

NCTM Standards: 1, 2, 3, 4, 5, 6, 7, 8

■ **A38**

To help a family escape on the Underground Railroad, we will work in teams. Each team will

Creating a "station house" for the family to hide in.
Have a "conductor" meet the family and bring it to the station house.
Locate a town where the station house will be. The family is coming up from South Carolina and wants to get to Canada.
Make a 3-D map of the route before the escape begins.

Your *station house* needs to

Be able to stand
Be 5 inches high
Have a base area of 16 square inches
Have trees around it that are taller than the house
Have a door that opens
Have a porch light that is lit
Have twice as many windows as doors
Have a place where the family can hide

When your station house is finished, attach it to the large escape map.

After you decide on the general location of your station house, make a map showing

The name of a town where your station-house is located
The state the town is in
The obstacles the family must get around, like rivers, lakes, and forests

When your map is finished, attach it next to your station house on the large escape map.

Figure out *how many miles* the family must travel to get from your station house to the next, and *how long* this will take.

Figure out *how much food* the family will need for the trip to the next station house.

Teams will need to plan the escape. A journal of the adventures and hardships the family met within its travel will be passed from team to team. You will write your comments in the journal when you get it.

When the family is safe in Canada, teams will meet for a celebration!

NCTM Standards: 1, 2, 3, 4, 5, 6, 7, 8, 10

Bibliography

Arcidiacono, Michael, Debby Head, and Libby Pollet. 1995. *Opening Eyes to Mathematics, Vol. 3*. Portland, OR: Math Learning Center.

Baker, Dave, Cheryl Semple, and Tony Stead. 1990. *How Big Is the Moon?: Whole-Maths in Action*. Portsmouth, NH: Heinemann.

Baretta-Lorton, Mary. 1995. *Math Their Way*. Menlo Park, CA: Addison-Wesley.

Bennett, Albert, and Linda Foreman. 1995. *Visual Mathematics, Course I*. Portland, OR: Math Learning Center.

Burk, Donna, Allyn Snider, and Paula Symonds. 1991. *Math Excursions: Project-Based Mathematics*. Portsmouth, NH: Heinemann.

Burns, Marilyn. 1988. *Math: Facing an American Phobia*. Sausalito, CA: Math Solutions.

———. 1992. *About Teaching Mathematics*. Sausalito, CA: Math Solutions.

Clement, Rod. 1991. *Counting on Frank*. Milwaukee, WI: Gareth Stevens.

Countryman, Joan. 1992. *Writing to Learn Mathematics*. Portsmouth, NH: Heinemann.

Hoose, Phillip. 1993. *It's Our World, Too!* Boston: Little, Brown.

Hubbard, Ruth. 1996. *A Workshop of the Possible: Nurturing Children's Creative Development*. York, ME: Stenhouse.

Hubbard, Ruth Shagoury, and Karen Ernst, eds. 1996. *New Entries: Learning by Writing and Drawing*. Portsmouth, NH: Heinemann.

Kamii, Constance, Barbara A. Lewis, and Sally Jones Livingston. 1993. Primary Arithmetic: Children Inventing Their Own Procedures. *Arithmetic Teacher* (December).

Lasky, Kathryn. 1994. *The Librarian Who Measured the Earth.* Boston: Little, Brown.

Meier, Deborah. 1995. *The Power of Their Ideas.* Boston: Beacon Press.

Mills, Heidi, Timothy O'Keefe, and David Whitin. 1990. *Mathematics in the Making.* Portsmouth, NH: Heinemann.

Mokros, Jan. 1996. *Beyond Facts and Flashcards: Exploring Math with Your Kids.* Portsmouth, NH: Heinemann.

National Council of Teachers of Mathematics. 1989. *Curriculum and Evaluation Standards for School Mathematics.* Reston, VA: NCTM.

Ohanian, Susan. 1992. *Garbage Pizzas, Patchwork Quilts, and Math Magic: Stories About Teachers Who Love to Teach and Children Who Love to Learn.* New York: W. H. Freeman.

Ostrow, Jill. 1995. *A Room with a Different View: First Through Third Graders Build Community and Create Curriculum.* York, ME: Stenhouse.

Parker, Ruth E. 1993. *Mathematical Power: Lessons from a Classroom.* Portsmouth, NH: Heinemann.

Perl, Teri. 1993. *Women and Numbers: Lives of Women Mathematicians.* San Carlos, CA: Wide World.

Phillips, Richard. 1994. *Numbers: Facts, Figures, and Fiction.* Cambridge, UK: Cambridge University Press.

Power, Brenda. 1997. *Taking Note: Improving Your Observational Notetaking.* York, ME: Stenhouse.

Power, Brenda, and Kelly Chandler. 1998. *Well-Chosen Words: Narrative Assessments and Report Card Comments.* York, ME: Stenhouse.

Rowan, Thomas, and Barbara Bourne. 1994. *Thinking Like Mathematicians: Putting the K–4 NCTM Standards into Practice.* Portsmouth, NH: Heinemann.

Snider, Allyn, and Donna Burk. 1994. *Posing and Solving Problems with Story Boxes.* Portland, OR: Math Learning Center.

———. In press. *Bridges to Mathematics.* Portland, OR: Math Learning Center.

Whitin, David, and Sandra Wilde. 1992. *Read Any Good Math Lately?: Children's Books for Mathematical Learning.* Portsmouth, NH: Heinemann.

Zaslavsky, Claudia. 1995. *The Multicultural Math Classroom: Bringing in the World.* Portsmouth, NH: Heinemann.

2386